BIBLE ATLAS

& COMPANION

CHRISTOPHER D. HUDSON
General Editor

DAVID BARRETT
Cartographer

TODD BOLEN
Photographer

BARBOUR
PUBLISHING

Bible Atlas & Companion © 2008 by Barbour Publishing

ISBN 978-1-59789-779-2

Satellite terrain imagery produced with data provided by the Global Land Cover Facility, http://www.landcover.org. Author: MDA Federal 2004. Landsat GeoCover 2000/ETM+ Edition Mosaics. Sioux Falls, South Dakota: USGS.

All elevation data was created from data supplied by Shuttle Radar Topography Mission (SRTM), a project of the National Aeronautics and Space Administration (NASA). A full description of this data can be found at http://www.usgs.gov.

Photo and Illustration Credits
All maps created by David Barrett (www.BibleMapper.com).
All photos taken from the library of Todd Bolen (www.BiblePlaces.com).
Special acknowledgement is made for the following images:
Page 28: Library of Congress, Prints & Photographs Division, LC-DIG-matpc-06959
Page 92: British Museum © Copyright the Trustees of The British Museum.
Page 110: British Museum © Copyright the Trustees of The British Museum.
Page 126: Istanbul Archaeological Museum, Istanbul.

Published by Barbour Publishing, Inc., P.O. Box 719 Uhrichsville, Ohio 44683, www.barbourbooks.com

Our mission is to publish and distribute inspirational products offering exceptional value and biblical encouragement to the masses.

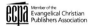
Member of the
Evangelical Christian
Publishers Association

Printed in China

CONTENTS

DEDICATION

To Caleb, Ryan, and Analiese.

The Bible is the most important book in the world. I hope books like this one help you understand it a little bit better.

INTRODUCTION

When Moses, Ezra, or Luke wrote books that later became part of the Bible, they had no way of envisioning readers living in the twenty-first century. As they wrote, they probably had their own children, grandchildren, and even great-grandchildren in mind—people they knew would understand the regional and geographical references in their writings.

For Bible readers today, however, thousands of years have passed, and those references have become obscure. And beyond the years, thousands of miles now separate most readers from the original locations of these stories, so we are not able to envision the landscapes and geography involved. When the Bible refers to the mountains of Israel, for example, we probably envision what we expect the mountains to look like. When we read about the countryside where Jesus preached, we may picture fields similar to those located near our homes.

Most of the time, those preconceived images aren't accurate. When David hid from Saul at En Gedi, he wasn't hiding in a charming, comfortable cave. When Joshua ambushed the Philistines, he didn't sneak up quietly on a grassy, gentle trail. And when the people rallied for war, they prepared to fight their enemies over difficult and rocky terrain—scenes difficult to imagine for modern readers who only know highly technological warfare.

This book can change the way you read the Bible. The photos in this book, which were taken exclusively from the collection of Todd Bolen, help give readers a more accurate picture of the colors, landscapes, and terrain of Bible lands. The maps, created by brilliant cartographer David Barrett, help today's reader understand what it was like for Jesus, Joshua, and the people of Israel to crisscross a country about the size of New Jersey—usually by foot.

To help your Bible reading and study, we've arranged these pages so they follow the order of the Bible's books. By arranging the maps and images this way, we hope this book can provide some of the context and insight the original readers of the Bible would have had.

Christopher D. Hudson
General Editor

INTRODUCTORY MAPS

THE HOLY LAND TODAY

Modern-day Israel became a state after Britain withdrew from Palestine in 1948. The United Nations voted to establish two states in the region: one Jewish, one Arab. While Israel accepted the plan and declared her independence, the local Arabs and other regional nations rejected the proposal.

Since its foundation in this modern era, the small Jewish state has fought a series of wars against hostile Arab neighbors—finally signing a peace treaty with Egypt in 1979 and Jordan in 1994. Today, significant conflict remains with the Palestinians (who live primarily in the West Bank and Gaza Strip). With few natural resources, Israel has built its economy on technology, tourism, and national defense.

The population living in Israel numbers about seven million.

Israel is one of the few countries in the region whose citizens participate in a democratic electoral process, a free economy, and freedom of the press.

The holiest place in Israel is the Temple Mount, which remains under Muslim control. It holds religious significance for Jewish, Christian, and Muslim worshipers alike. The photo shows a Jewish man praying at the "Western Wall." This portion of the wall is a sacred part of the compound wall of the Jewish temple that the Romans destroyed in AD 70. Millions of people of all faiths (mostly Jewish) have prayed at this site, often sliding slips of paper containing prayers between the rocks of the wall.

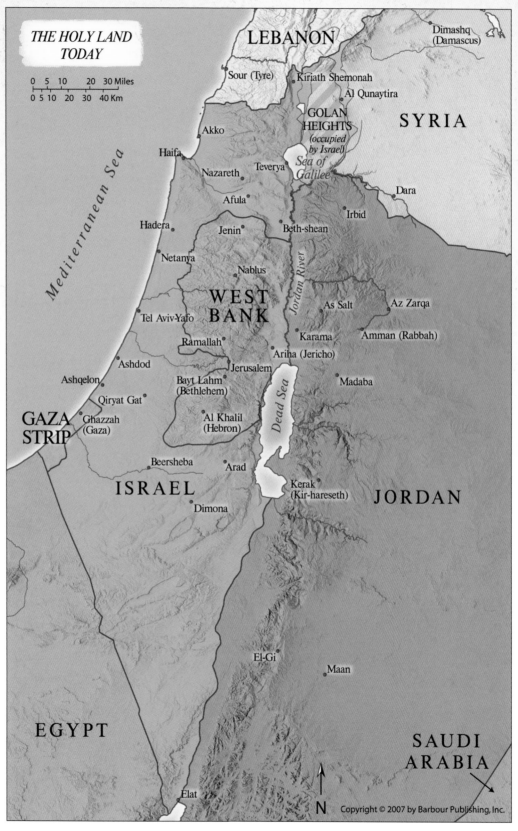

THE HOLY LAND TODAY

0 5 10   20   30 Miles
0 5 10   20   30   40 Km

LEBANON

Dimashq (Damascus)

Sour (Tyre)

Kiriath Shemonah

Al Qunaytira

GOLAN HEIGHTS (occupied by Israel)

SYRIA

Akko

Haifa

Nazareth

Teverya

Sea of Galilee

Dara

Afula

Irbid

Mediterranean Sea

Hadera

Jenin

Beth-shean

Netanya

Nablus

Jordan River

WEST BANK

As Salt

Az Zarqa

Tel Aviv-Yafo

Ramallah

Karama

Amman (Rabbah)

Ashdod

Jerusalem

Ariha (Jericho)

Ashqelon

Bayt Lahm (Bethlehem)

Madaba

Qiryat Gat

GAZA STRIP

Ghazzah (Gaza)

Al Khalil (Hebron)

Dead Sea

Beersheba

Arad

ISRAEL

Kerak (Kir-haresheth)

JORDAN

Dimona

EGYPT

El-Gi

Maan

SAUDI ARABIA

N

Elat

Copyright © 2007 by Barbour Publishing, Inc.

GEOGRAPHY OF THE HOLY LAND

The climate of Israel varies greatly depending on the time of year and the location. Areas in southern Israel, such as the Negev, are very dry—receiving less than ten inches of rain each year (see photo at bottom). Vegetation in this area is sparse, being mostly populated with wild desert scrub and occasional acacia trees, which spot the landscape (see photo on page 26).

In the northern region, rain is much more plentiful—especially during the months of December through February—which makes the landscape significantly more lush than in the south (see photo at left). Snowfall is rare but does occur in the Golan Heights region.

The varied climate and landscape became a backdrop used by biblical writers. Below are two examples:

THE LUSH NORTHERN REGION:
For the LORD your God is bringing you into a good land—a land with streams and pools of water, with springs flowing in the valleys and hills; a land with wheat and barley, vines and fig trees, pomegranates, olive oil and honey; a land where bread will not be scarce and you will lack nothing; a land where the rocks are iron and you can dig copper out of the hills (Deuteronomy 8:7–9).

JUDEAN DESERT:
O God, you are my God, earnestly I seek you; my soul thirsts for you, my body longs for you, in a dry and weary land where there is no water (Psalm 63:1).

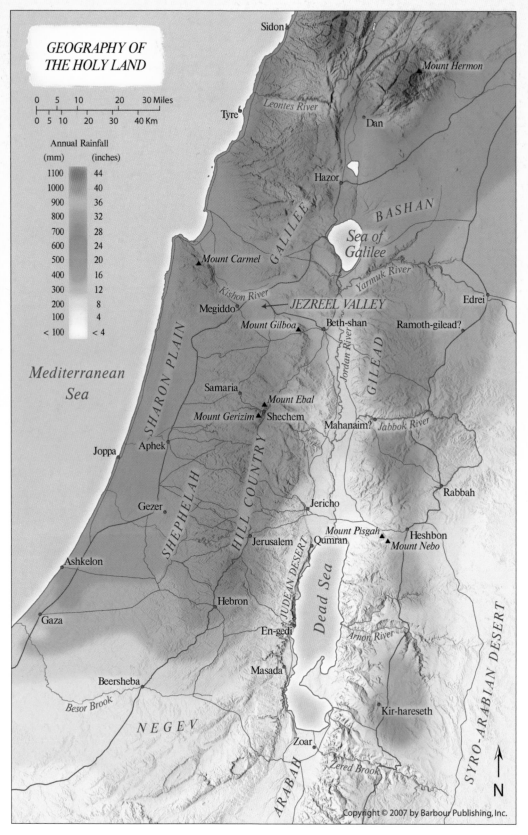

GEOGRAPHY OF THE HOLY LAND

```
0    5   10      20     30 Miles
0  5 10   20    30    40 Km
```

Annual Rainfall

(mm)	(inches)
1100	44
1000	40
900	36
800	32
700	28
600	24
500	20
400	16
300	12
200	8
100	4
< 100	< 4

Sidon

Mount Hermon

Leontes River

Tyre

Dan

Hazor

GALILEE

BASHAN

Sea of Galilee

Mount Carmel

Yarmuk River

Kishon River

JEZREEL VALLEY

Edrei

Megiddo

Mount Gilboa

Beth-shan

Ramoth-gilead?

Samaria

Mount Ebal

GILEAD

Jordan River

Mediterranean Sea

SHARON PLAIN

Mount Gerizim

Shechem

Mahanaim?

Jabbok River

Joppa

Aphek

SHEPHELAH

HILL COUNTRY

Rabbah

Gezer

Jericho

Jerusalem

Qumran

Mount Pisgah

Heshbon

Mount Nebo

Ashkelon

JUDEAN DESERT

Dead Sea

Hebron

Gaza

En-gedi

Arnon River

SYRO-ARABIAN DESERT

Masada

Beersheba

Kir-hareseth

Besor Brook

NEGEV

Zoar

ARABAH

Zered Brook

N

THE LANDS OF THE BIBLE TODAY

Though only the approximate size of New Jersey, the land of Israel is filled with people of many religions and cultures.

Founded as a Jewish homeland, the country of Israel's population today consists of both those who identify themselves as Jewish (76%) and those who practice Islam (16%). The remaining residents practice Christianity, Baha'i, Druze, and other world religions. And while many identify themselves as "Jewish," most do so because of their Hebrew descent not because of their strict religious practices.

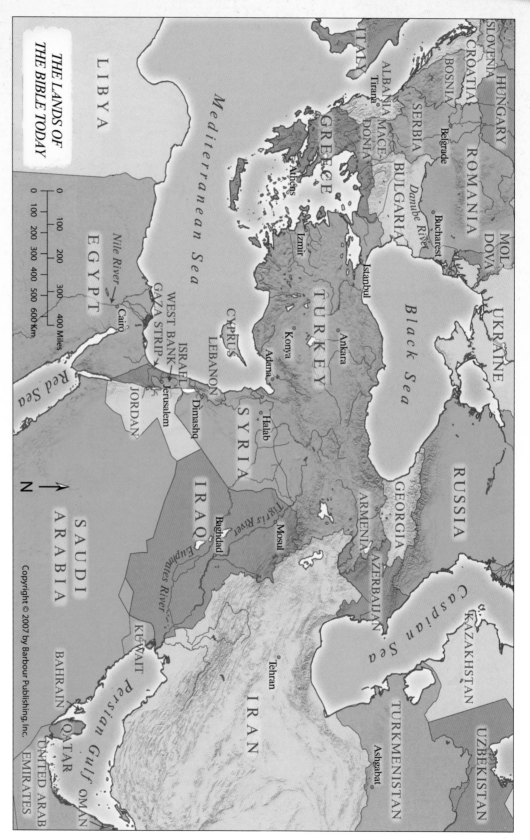

THE LANDS OF
THE BIBLE TODAY

Copyright © 2007 by Barbour Publishing, Inc.

THE PENTATEUCH

Hazor

Mediterranean Sea

Megiddo
Beth-shan

ISRAEL

Jerusalem
Jericho

Gaza Hebron

JUDAH

MOAB

Beersheba

Alexandria

LOWER
Zoan
Sin (Pelusium)

EGYPT
Rameses
Migdol
Tahpanhes
Pithom?

Pi-beseth (Bubastis)

GOSHEN
Way to Shur

Brook of
Egypt?

On (Heliopolis)

EDOM

Great Pyramids

SINAI

Elath

Memphis
(Noph)

Ezion-geber?

PENINSULA

(claimed by Egypt)

MIDIAN

Oxyrhynchus

Rephidim?

Mount Sinai?
(J. Musa)

Nile River

Red Sea

Abydos

NATIONS OF THE ANCIENT WORLD

The Bible's account of the global flood reports the story of Noah and the world-wide devastation he witnessed. With everyone else dead, Noah and his family were the only people left to repopulate the earth. Thus, every person on earth is descended from the three sons of Noah: Ham, Shem, and Japheth. The map on the next page captures the likely location of each people group and their probable patriarch.

The time line below highlights some of the biblical history that occurred between Noah and the time of the Hebrew kings.

2165 BC	Abraham is born.
2070 BC	Sodom and Gomorrah are destroyed.
1700 BC	The life of Job? (Exact timing is unknown.)
1922 BC	Jacob marries both Rachel and Leah.
1805 BC	Joseph dies.
1526 BC	Moses is born.
1450 BC	God speaks to Moses from the burning bush.
1400 BC	The time of the Judges begins.
1050 BC	Saul becomes the first king of Israel.

The biblical timeline continues on page 96.

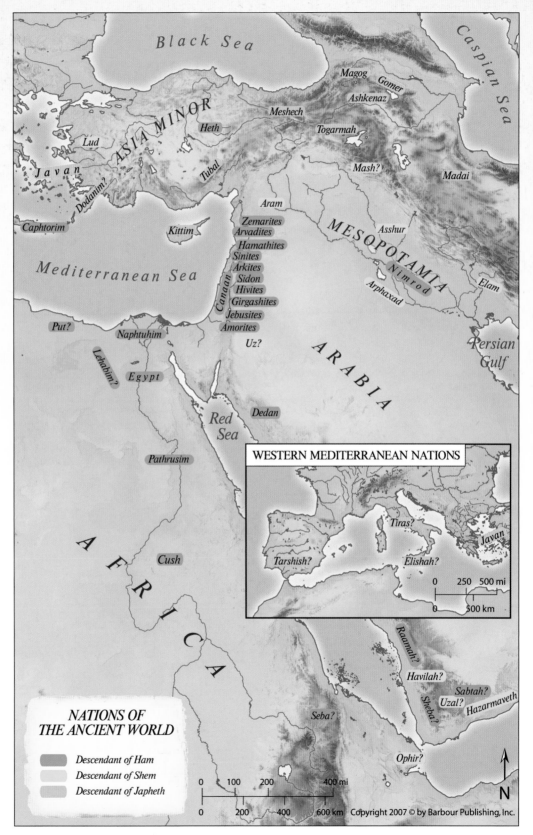

Black Sea

Caspian Sea

Magog

Gomer

Ashkenaz

Meshech

Heth

Togarmah

ASIA MINOR

Lud

Javan

Tubal

Mash?

Madai

Dodanim?

Aram

Caphtorim

Kittim

Zemarites

Arvadites

MESOPOTAMIA

Asshur

Elam

Hamathites

Sinites

Nimrod

Mediterranean Sea

Arkites

Sidon

Arphaxad

Hivites

Canaan

Girgashites

Jebusites

Put?

Amorites

Persian
Gulf

Naphtuhim

Uz?

A R A B I A

Lehabim?

Egypt

Red
Sea

Dedan

Pathrusim

WESTERN MEDITERRANEAN NATIONS

Tiras?

Javan

Tarshish?

Elishah?

0 250 500 mi

0 500 km

A F R I C A

Cush

Raamah?

Havilah?

Sabtah?

Uzal?

Sheba?

Hazarmaveth

Seba?

Ophir?

NATIONS OF
THE ANCIENT WORLD

Descendant of Ham

Descendant of Shem

Descendant of Japheth

0 100 200 400 mi

0 200 400 600 km   Copyright 2007 © by Barbour Publishing, Inc.

N

NEAR EAST DURING THE TIME OF THE PATRIARCHS

The story of God's people begins with Abram (later known as Abraham) in the land of Ur. While Abram was living in the region known as Babylonia, God appeared to him and instructed him to travel to Canaan—known today as Israel. This thousand-mile journey became a major turning point in human history.

The story of Abraham (Genesis 12–25) includes God's promise of a son whose descendants would populate the promised land. During Abraham's lifetime, he lived in Canaan, moved to Egypt, and returned to Canaan.

Throughout the centuries, Abraham has been a key figure in the Jewish, Christian, and Islamic religions. His central place in the faith of many has caused Abraham's traditional burial site (located in Hebron) to be seen as one of the most holy places in the Middle East (see photo). This location is believed to be the burial place of Abraham, Sarah, Isaac, Rebekah, Jacob, and Leah. The building which now houses this location was built by Herod the Great.

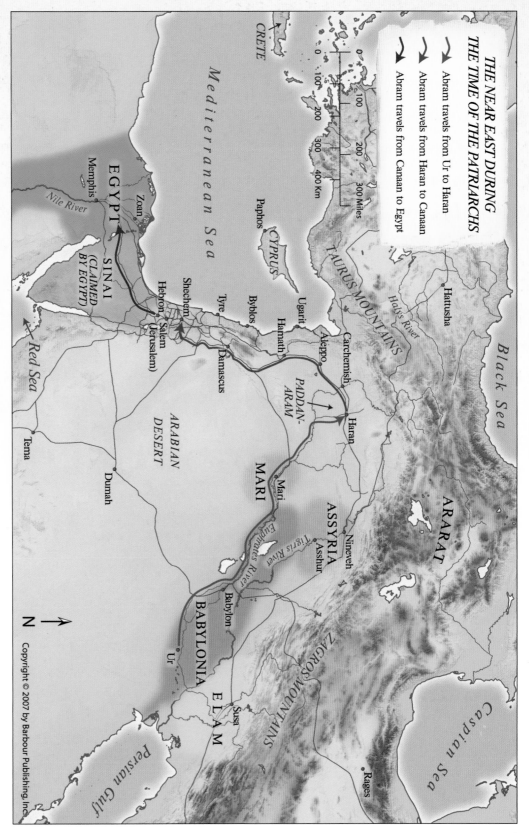

THE NEAR EAST DURING
THE TIME OF THE PATRIARCHS

Abram travels from Ur to Haran

Abram travels from Haran to Canaan

Abram travels from Canaan to Egypt

0   100   200   300   400 Km

0   100   200   300 Miles

Black Sea

Caspian Sea

CRETE

Mediterranean Sea

CYPRUS

Paphos

EGYPT

Memphis

Nile River

Zoan

SINAI
(CLAIMED
BY EGYPT)

Red Sea

Hebron
Salem
(Jerusalem)

Shechem

Tyre

Byblos

Hamath

Ugarit

Aleppo

Carchemish

TAURUS MOUNTAINS

Habis River

Hattusha

Damascus

PADDAN-
ARAM

Haran

ARABIAN
DESERT

MARI

Mari

Euphrates River

Tigris River

ASSYRIA

Asshur

Nineveh

ARARAT

ZAGROS MOUNTAINS

Tema

Dumah

BABYLONIA

Babylon

Ur

ELAM

Susa

Rages

N

Persian Gulf

Copyright © 2007 by Barbour Publishing, Inc.

19

CANAAN DURING THE TIME OF THE PATRIARCHS

Abraham's nephew, Lot, lived near the cities of Sodom and Gomorrah. When a coalition of four kings conquered the cities, they carried off Lot and his family as captives of war (see Genesis 14). When Abraham heard that Lot had been taken captive, Abraham mobilized his own militia, pursued the kings, and won Lot's freedom.

As nomads, Abraham and his sons built their wealth through large flocks. The photo contains a scene of herds in the land of Beersheba, similar to the herds that would have grazed during the time of Abraham and his descendants.

Two generations after Abraham, Jacob and Esau became rivals for their father Isaac's blessing and wealth. In order to receive the blessing that Isaac planned to give to Esau, Jacob deceived his father. This enraged Esau, and caused Jacob to flee his home and seek refuge with his uncle Laban for twenty years before returning to Canaan. Esau pursued Jacob—but their meeting ended with reconciliation (see Genesis 32–33).

Throughout the stories of the patriarchs, common themes include faith, prayer, and worship. Frequently, the patriarchs made stops along their journeys to build altars to God. The map to the right records the locations of many of these altars.

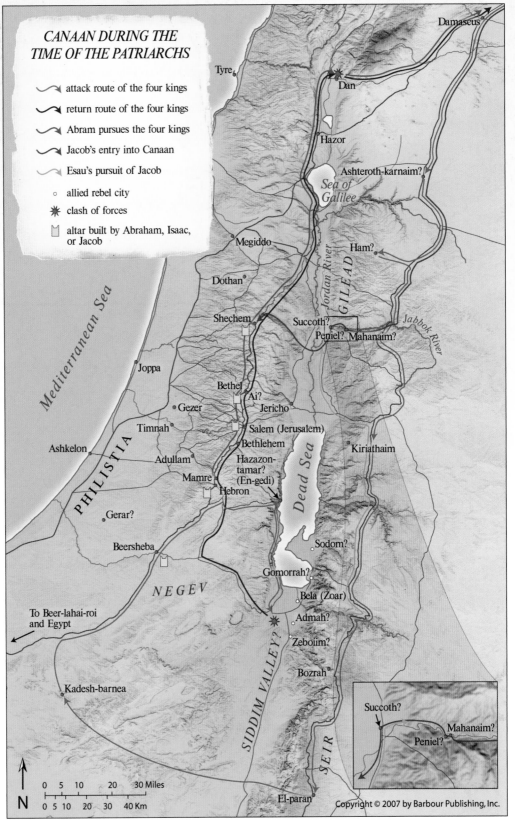

CANAAN DURING THE TIME OF THE PATRIARCHS

- ⌇ attack route of the four kings
- ⌇ return route of the four kings
- ⌇ Abram pursues the four kings
- ⌇ Jacob's entry into Canaan
- ⌇ Esau's pursuit of Jacob
- ○ allied rebel city
- ✳ clash of forces
- ⛩ altar built by Abraham, Isaac, or Jacob

Damascus

Tyre

Dan

Hazor

Ashteroth-karnaim?

Sea of Galilee

Jordan River

GILEAD

Ham?

Megiddo

Dothan

Shechem

Succoth?

Peniel? Mahanaim?

Jabbok River

Mediterranean Sea

Joppa

Bethel

Ai?

Jericho

Gezer

Salem (Jerusalem)

Timnah

Bethlehem

Kiriathaim

Ashkelon

Adullam

Hazazon-
tamar?
(En-gedi)

PHILISTIA

Mamre

Hebron

Dead Sea

Gerar?

Beersheba

Sodom?

NEGEV

Gomorrah?

Bela (Zoar)

To Beer-lahai-roi
and Egypt

Admah?

Zeboiim?

SIDDIM VALLEY?

Bozrah

Kadesh-barnea

SEIR

Succoth?

Mahanaim?

Peniel?

0 5 10   20   30 Miles

N

0 5 10   20   30   40 Km

El-paran

Copyright © 2007 by Barbour Publishing, Inc.

EGYPT IN THE BIBLE

Located to the southwest of the promised land, Egypt frequently enters into the biblical narrative as the setting for key stories. Below are some of the many occurrences of Egypt in the Bible:

- Genesis 12: Abram moves to Egypt to escape a famine in the land.
- Genesis 37: Joseph is sold into Egyptian slavery.
- Genesis 47: Jacob and his sons move to the land of Goshen, where their descendants live for four hundred years—eventually becoming slaves of the Egyptians.
- Exodus 13–19: Moses leads the people out of Egyptian slavery to Mount Sinai (see page 24).
- 1 Kings 3: King Solomon makes an alliance with Egypt.
- 1 Kings 11: Jeroboam lives in Egyptian exile until the death of King Solomon.
- 2 Kings 23 and 2 Chronicles 35: King Neco of Egypt battles Josiah (see page 92).
- 2 Chronicles 12: King Shishak of Egypt attacks Jerusalem.
- Matthew 2: Mary, Joseph, and Jesus flee to Egypt.
- Acts 8: The Ethiopian eunuch travels through Egypt on his way back to Ethiopia (see page 148).

Historians agree that the great pyramids of Egypt (see photo) were built about one thousand years before the Israelite people initially moved to Goshen (see Genesis 47). While the pyramids are never mentioned in the Bible, the view of the impressive buildings may have been shared by many of the biblical characters who sojourned in Egypt.

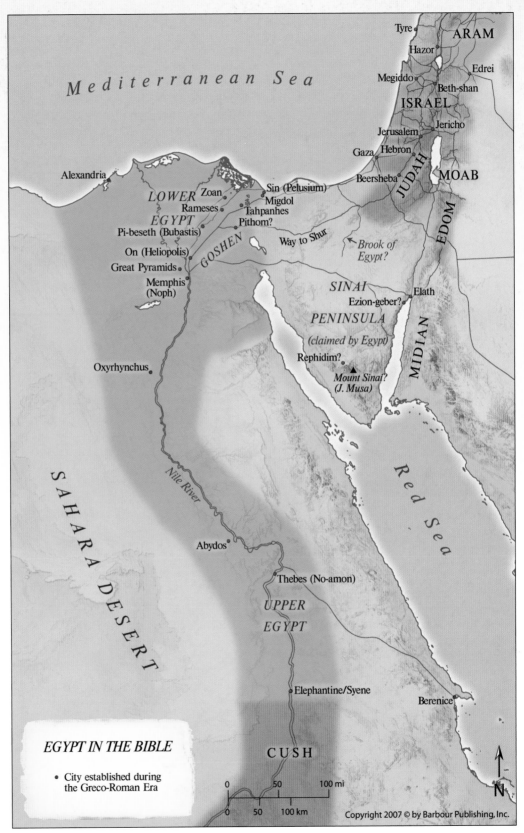

Mediterranean Sea

Tyre

ARAM

Hazor

Edrei

Megiddo

Beth-shan

ISRAEL

Jerusalem

Jericho

Gaza   Hebron

JUDAH   MOAB

Alexandria

Sin (Pelusium)

Beersheba

LOWER   Zoan

EGYPT   Migdol

Rameses   Tahpanhes

EDOM

Pithom?

Pi-beseth (Bubastis)

GOSHEN   Way to Shur   Brook of
Egypt?

On (Heliopolis)

SINAI

Great Pyramids

Ezion-geber?   Elath

Memphis
(Noph)

PENINSULA

(claimed by Egypt)

MIDIAN

Oxyrhynchus

Rephidim?

Mount Sinai?
(J. Musa)

Red Sea

Nile River

SAHARA DESERT

Abydos

Thebes (No-amon)

UPPER

EGYPT

Elephantine/Syene

Berenice

EGYPT IN THE BIBLE

CUSH

• City established during
the Greco-Roman Era

0   50   100 mi

N

0   50   100 km

Copyright 2007 © by Barbour Publishing, Inc.

THE EXODUS FROM EGYPT

While Sunday school teachers refer to the Red Sea as the location of Moses' great confrontation with Pharaoh's army, the Hebrew language found within the book of Exodus is less precise. Because most of the Israelite people were enslaved in the region of Goshen, the location of the event may have been the actual Red Sea or one of the lakes to the north.

After God miraculously delivered the Israelites from the pursuing Egyptians, Moses led the people south to Mount Sinai, which most likely was located in the southern end of the Sinai Peninsula. It was at Mount Sinai that the people received instructions from God that included the Ten Commandments (see Exodus 20).

While Michelangelo's Moses (see photo) depicts a young man, Moses took leadership of the people of Israel when he was eighty years old. He had spent the previous forty years living as a nomadic shepherd in dry, arid regions. It's likely that during these decades in the wilderness, Moses grew in his faith and learned practical lessons about living in barren climates. This skill would prove useful as he led the people out of the fertile region of Goshen into the dry wilderness they would end up inhabiting for forty years.

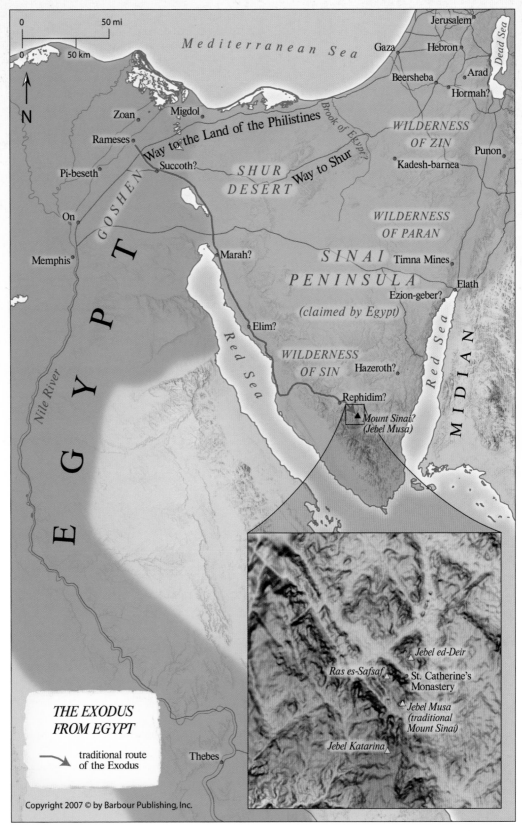

0   50 mi
0   50 km

N

Mediterranean Sea

Jerusalem

Dead Sea

Gaza   Hebron

Beersheba   Arad

Hormah?

Zoan   Migdol

Way to the Land of the Philistines

Brook of Egypt?

Rameses

*WILDERNESS
OF ZIN*

Punon

Pi-beseth   Succoth?   *SHUR
DESERT*   Way to Shur   Kadesh-barnea

GOSHEN

*WILDERNESS
OF PARAN*

On

E G Y P T   *S I N A I*   Timna Mines

Marah?   *P E N I N S U L A*   Elath

Memphis   *(claimed by Egypt)*   Ezion-geber?

Red Sea   Elim?   *Red Sea*

*WILDERNESS
OF SIN*   Hazeroth?   *M I D I A N*

Nile River   Rephidim?

▲ *Mount Sinai?
(Jebel Musa)*

Jebel ed-Deir

Ras es-Safsaf   △ St. Catherine's
Monastery

△ *Jebel Musa
(traditional
Mount Sinai)*

Jebel Katarina △

THE EXODUS
FROM EGYPT

→ traditional route
of the Exodus

Thebes

EVENTS IN THE WILDERNESS

The Israelites' route through the Wilderness of Sin was through dry, uneven landscapes that were occasionally spotted with acacia trees. The dense wood of these trees yielded a durable product that the Israelites used to build the tabernacle and its accessories (see Exodus 25–27).

This photograph was taken in the southern Sinai Peninsula, where most scholars believe the Wilderness of Sin was located. (This area was named for a regional deity, not because of a sinful act.) The difficult and arid terrain makes it understandable why the Israelites often complained about their constant lack of food and water. Here in this wilderness, God began to provide daily manna for the people to eat (Exodus 16).

While the people camped at Kadesh-barnea, Moses sent twelve spies into the promised land through a southern route (Numbers 13), and the resulting story is well-known: Ten spies said that the enemies were too powerful to defeat, while two spies (Joshua and Caleb) pressed the people to trust God for victory. After the people sided with the ten spies, God pronounced His severe judgment (Numbers 14). In an effort to skirt God's discipline, a contingent of men armed themselves in a rash effort to conquer the promised land. Against Moses' advice, these Israelite soldiers marched north and were soundly defeated by the Amalekites and Canaanites (Numbers 14:40–45).

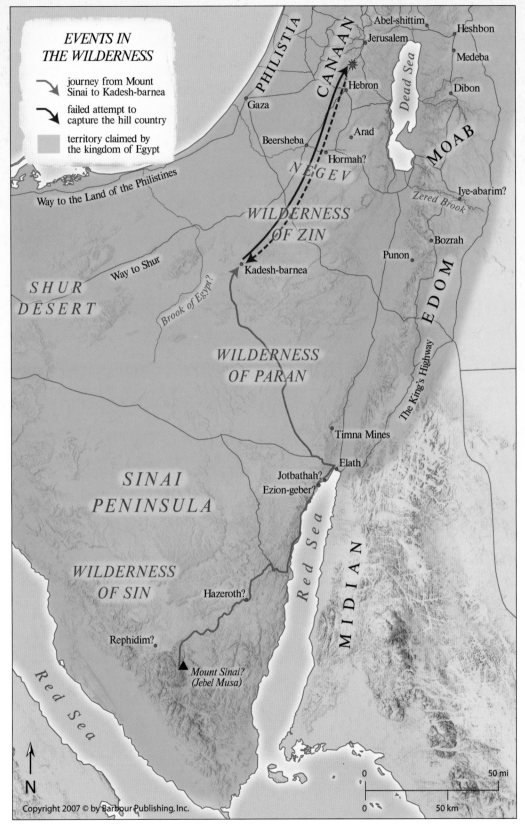

EVENTS IN
THE WILDERNESS

journey from Mount
Sinai to Kadesh-barnea

failed attempt to
capture the hill country

territory claimed by
the kingdom of Egypt

PHILISTIA

CANAAN

Abel-shittim

Jerusalem

Heshbon

Medeba

Hebron

Dead Sea

Dibon

Gaza

Arad

MOAB

Beersheba

Hormah?

N E G E V

Iye-abarim?

Zered Brook

WILDERNESS
OF ZIN

Bozrah

Punon

SHUR
DESERT

Way to Shur

Way to the Land of the Philistines

Brook of Egypt?

Kadesh-barnea

EDOM

WILDERNESS
OF PARAN

The King's Highway

Timna Mines

Elath

SINAI
PENINSULA

Jotbathah?

Ezion-geber?

Red Sea

MIDIAN

WILDERNESS
OF SIN

Hazeroth?

Rephidim?

Mount Sinai?
(Jebel Musa)

Red Sea

N

0   50 mi

0   50 km

Copyright 2007 © by Barbour Publishing, Inc.

JOURNEY TO THE PROMISED LAND

Because of the Israelites' rebellion, God condemned them to live in the wilderness for forty years. During this time, every living adult (with the exception of Joshua and Caleb) died because of their disobedience to God. Joshua, Caleb, and the children (who would grow into adults during this time) would be the only ones to enter the promised land (Numbers 14).

Toward the end of their journey, the Israelites requested permission from King Sihon of the Amorites to peacefully pass through his territory. Not only did he refuse, he also mobilized his army and attacked God's people. The Israelites soundly defeated the Amorites, as well as King Og of Bashan (Numbers 21).

The people finally arrived at Abel-shittim and received God's instructions for taking the land. This was the final leg of their journey with Moses as their leader. Before Moses died, however, God directed him to climb Mount Nebo. From this height of 3,300 feet, Moses received a clear view of the promised land (see photo showing this same view). Moses died on top of the mountain and was buried by God Himself in a secret grave (Deuteronomy 34). Joshua assumed leadership of the people and led the conquest of Canaan.

JOURNEY TO THE PROMISED LAND

Probable route of the Israelites' journey to Abel-shittim

King Sihon attacks the Israelites

Israelite battle missions

King Og attacks the Israelites

Land taken from Og and Sihon

0   10   20   30 mi

0   20   40 km

Mediterranean Sea

Hazor

BASHAN

Sea of Galilee

Ashtaroth

Edrei

Yarmuk River

Megiddo

Beth-shan

Ramoth-gilead

Jordan River

GILEAD

Shechem

Jabbok River

AMMON

Joppa

PLAINS OF MOAB

Jazer?

Rabbah

Jericho

Abel-shittim

Beth-jeshimoth

Heshbon

Jebus (Jerusalem)

Mount Nebo

Moses dies

Dead Sea

Medeba

Jahaz?

Dibon

Hebron

Aroer

Kedemoth?

Arnon River

Gaza

Ar?

Gerar?

M O A B

Beersheba

Arad

Kir-hareseth

Hormah?

Zoar

Zered Brook

Iye-abarim?

N E G E V

Tamar?

Besor Brook

Bozrah

Aaron dies

Mount Hor?

Punon

E D O M

Kadesh-barnea

WILDERNESS OF ZIN

The King's Highway

A R A B A H

ARABIAN DESERT

WILDERNESS OF PARAN

Timna Mines

Elath

Jotbathah

Ezion-geber?

Red Sea

N

Copyright © 2007 by Barbour Publishing, Inc.

29

BALAAM BLESSES ISRAEL

After hearing about the Israelites' swift military successes, the people of Moab grew fearful of their new, powerful neighbors. Rather than pursue direct military action, King Balak of Moab sought divine help.

Balak sent emissaries from Moab and neighboring Midian to recruit a well-known soothsayer named Balaam. After receiving visions from God, Balaam agreed to travel to Moab and meet with the king.

While on their way to Moab, Balaam's donkey began to act strangely. The beast refused to stay on the path and even crushed Balaam's foot against a wall. In anger and frustration, Balaam beat the animal, which responded by talking in a human voice.

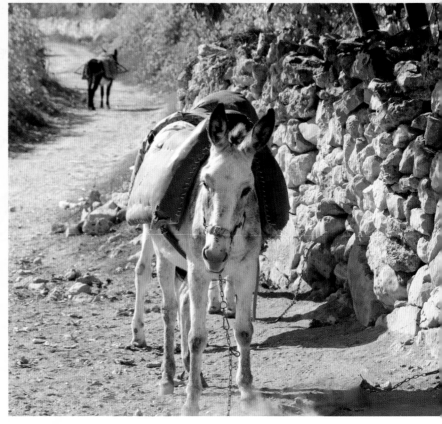

Upon hearing the voice, Balaam's eyes were opened—and he saw that God's angel was blocking the path. The donkey had actually saved Balaam's life. With a new respect for the power of God, Balaam continued on the southern journey to Moab.

Balaak received Balaam and together they hiked along some taller mountains so that the king and soothsayer could view the Israelites firsthand.

Balaam, following specific instructions from the one true God, refused to curse the people but blessed them instead. Read the intriguing story of Balaam and his talking donkey in Numbers 22–24.

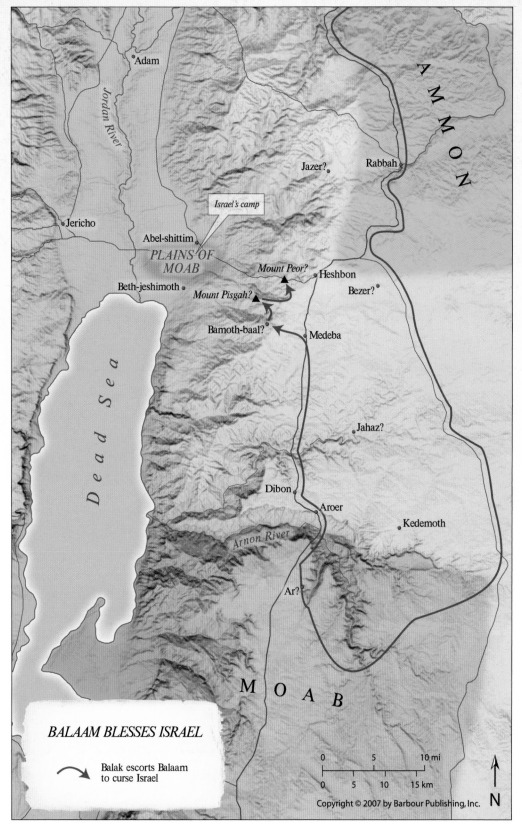

Adam

Jordan River

Jazer?

Rabbah

A
M
M
O
N

Jericho

Israel's camp

Abel-shittim

PLAINS OF
MOAB

Mount Peor?

Heshbon

Bezer?

Beth-jeshimoth

Mount Pisgah?

Bamoth-baal?

Medeba

Dead Sea

Jahaz?

Dibon

Aroer

Kedemoth

Arnon River

Ar?

M O A B

BALAAM BLESSES ISRAEL

Balak escorts Balaam
to curse Israel

| 0 | 5 | 10 mi |
| 0 | 5 | 10 | 15 km |

N

BOUNDARIES OF THE PROMISED LAND

The southern section of the Dead Sea (also known as the Salt Sea) pictured here became a natural boundary between the people of Israel and the people of Moab. God carefully described the extent of Israel's promised land using features such as the Dead Sea, the Jordan River, and the Mediterranean Sea (see the details recorded in Numbers 34).

As the people approached the promised land, the tribes of Manasseh, Gad, and Reuben realized that the plains on the eastern side of the Jordan River would be very suitable for their large herds. While not originally part of the boundaries promised by God, Moses agreed that they could acquire this eastern land as their own (Numbers 32).

The map to the right shows that the land that was ultimately occupied by the Israelites under Joshua's leadership was only a portion of the land that God had originally promised them in Numbers 34. Rather than being an act of disobedience, this more likely demonstrated that the people knew they didn't have the population or resources to settle the entire promised area. They lived with smaller boundaries, trusting God to fulfill His promises of Exodus 23:29–30, "But I will not drive [your enemies] out in a single year, because the land would become desolate and the wild animals too numerous for you. Little by little I will drive them out before you, until you have increased enough to take possession of the land."

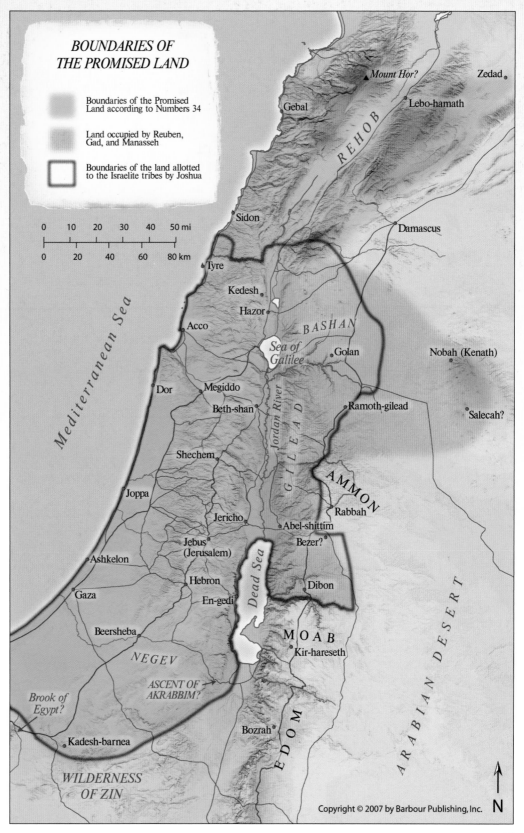

BOUNDARIES OF THE PROMISED LAND

Boundaries of the Promised Land according to Numbers 34

Land occupied by Reuben, Gad, and Manasseh

Boundaries of the land allotted to the Israelite tribes by Joshua

0   10   20   30   40   50 mi

0   20   40   60   80 km

Mediterranean Sea

REHOB

Mount Hor?

Zedad

Gebal

Lebo-hamath

Sidon

Damascus

Tyre

Kedesh

Hazor

BASHAN

Acco

Sea of Galilee

Golan

Nobah (Kenath)

Dor

Megiddo

Beth-shan

GILEAD

Ramoth-gilead

Salecah?

Jordan River

Shechem

AMMON

Joppa

Rabbah

Jericho

Abel-shittim

Jebus (Jerusalem)

Bezer?

Ashkelon

Hebron

Dibon

Gaza

En-gedi

Dead Sea

MOAB

Beersheba

Kir-hareseth

NEGEV

ASCENT OF AKRABBIM?

ARABIAN DESERT

Brook of Egypt?

Bozrah

EDOM

Kadesh-barnea

WILDERNESS OF ZIN

Copyright © 2007 by Barbour Publishing, Inc.

N

33

HISTORICAL AND POETICAL BOOKS

ISRAEL ENTERS THE PROMISED LAND

While action-minded readers enjoy reading about the conquests of Jericho and Ai (Joshua 6–8), the stories of Israel's spiritual stops during the journey are equally important.

After miraculously crossing the Jordan, the people of God immediately worshiped God by building an altar (Joshua 3–4).

After defeating Jericho and Ai, the people paused again to worship God. Following the instructions given by Moses (Deuteronomy 11:29 and Deuteronomy 27), one half of the people stood at Mt. Gerizim and one half stood at Mount Ebal and shouted specific blessings and curses according to Moses' instructions. With the people assembled, Joshua read the Law of Moses in its entirety to the people (Joshua 8:34–35).

God did not haphazardly select the site of this worship service. The historic city of Shechem lies between these mountains, and it was the first place in Canaan that Abraham built an altar after being promised that his descendants would inherit this land (Genesis 12:6–7).

Abraham's grandson Jacob settled at Shechem and built an altar after being reunited with Esau (Genesis 33:18–20). Additionally, Jacob's twelve sons lived here while grazing their flocks (Genesis 37:12–13). By worshiping in this place, the people celebrated that they had finally come home.

The photo on this page is a view of Mt. Ebal taken from Mt. Gerizim.

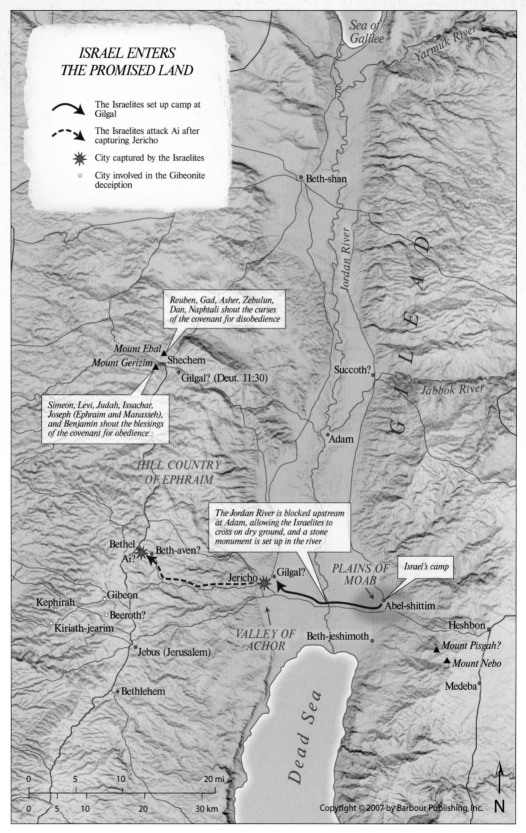

ISRAEL ENTERS THE PROMISED LAND

➤ The Israelites set up camp at Gilgal

➤ The Israelites attack Ai after capturing Jericho

✴ City captured by the Israelites

○ City involved in the Gibeonite deception

Sea of Galilee

Yarmuk River

Beth-shan

Jordan River

G I L E A D

Reuben, Gad, Asher, Zebulun, Dan, Naphtali shout the curses of the covenant for disobedience

Mount Ebal
Mount Gerizim ▲ Shechem

Gilgal? (Deut. 11:30)

Succoth?

Jabbok River

Simeon, Levi, Judah, Issachar, Joseph (Ephraim and Manasseh), and Benjamin shout the blessings of the covenant for obedience

Adam

HILL COUNTRY OF EPHRAIM

The Jordan River is blocked upstream at Adam, allowing the Israelites to cross on dry ground, and a stone monument is set up in the river

Bethel ✴
Ai? ✴ Beth-aven?

Jericho ✴ Gilgal?

PLAINS OF MOAB

Israel's camp

Kephirah ○ Gibeon

Beeroth?

Abel-shittim

Kiriath-jearim

Heshbon

VALLEY OF ACHOR

Beth-jeshimoth

▲ Mount Pisgah?

Jebus (Jerusalem)

▲ Mount Nebo

Bethlehem

Medeba

Dead Sea

0   5   10   20 mi
0   5   10   20   30 km

N

ISRAEL'S BATTLES FOR THE PROMISED LAND

The Bible records supernatural events that occurred as Israel conquered Jericho. Recent archaeological discoveries corroborate biblical events. Findings include:

- At the time the city fell, Jericho's mud brick walls unexpectedly collapsed in some areas (Joshua 6:20).
- Jericho's buildings were destroyed by fire (Joshua 6:24).
- The discovery of many storage jars filled with grain. This substantiates the biblical account that the battle took place after the spring harvest (Joshua 3:15) and that the people did not plunder the city (Joshua 6:18).
- A portion of the wall did not collapse. This is consistent with the belief that Rahab's house may have been part of the wall (Joshua 6:22). See photo.
- The city remained vacant for generations after this victory (Joshua 6:26).

Soon after these victories, the Gibeonites tricked the Israelites into making an alliance (Joshua 9). God used that alliance to provide a decisive battle against five Amorite kings (see the green lines). Once they defeated these kings, the Israelite army moved through the region and conquered the southern portion of the country (Joshua 10). Joshua and the armies regrouped in the city of Gilgal (Joshua 10:43).

After seeing their southern neighbors defeated, the Canaanite people in the north (represented by the blue lines) joined forces in a futile attempt to oppose the Israelites (Joshua 11). Joshua moved his armies from Gilgal and defeated these kings as well. An extensive catalogue of military victories can be found in Joshua 12.

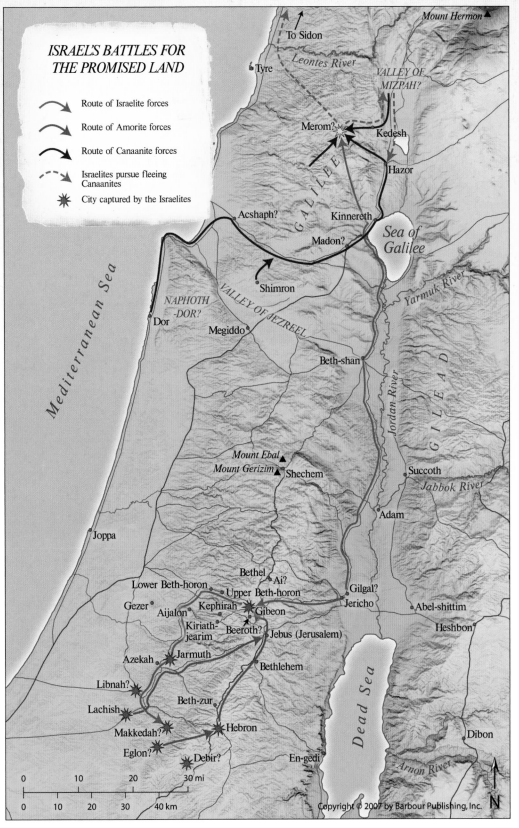

ISRAEL'S BATTLES FOR
THE PROMISED LAND

Route of Israelite forces

Route of Amorite forces

Route of Canaanite forces

Israelites pursue fleeing
Canaanites

City captured by the Israelites

Mount Hermon

To Sidon

Leontes River

VALLEY OF
MIZPAH?

Tyre

Merom?

Kedesh

Hazor

GALILEE

Acshaph?

Kinnereth

Madon?

Sea of
Galilee

Shimron

Yarmuk River

VALLEY OF MEZREEL

Mediterranean Sea

NAPHOTH
-DOR?

Dor

Megiddo

Beth-shan

Jordan River

GILEAD

Mount Ebal
Mount Gerizim

Shechem

Succoth

Jabbok River

Adam

Joppa

Bethel

Ai?

Lower Beth-horon

Upper Beth-horon

Gilgal?

Jericho

Abel-shittim

Gezer

Aijalon

Kephirah

Gibeon

Kiriath-
jearim

Beeroth?

Jebus (Jerusalem)

Heshbon

Bethlehem

Azekah

Jarmuth

Libnah?

Beth-zur

Dead Sea

Lachish

Makkedah?

Hebron

Eglon?

Debir?

Dibon

En-gedi

Arnon River

0   10   20   30 mi

0   10   20   30   40 km

Copyright © 2007 by Barbour Publishing, Inc.

N

THE TRIBAL ALLOTMENTS OF ISRAEL

Joshua 13–19 records the allotment of land granted to each tribe of Israel. The priestly tribe of Levi, however, did not receive a specific region as an inheritance. Rather, they received forty-eight cities scattered throughout the other tribal allotments—perhaps to make their spiritual influence felt throughout the whole nation (Joshua 21).

Joshua 20 records that six cities were designated as cities of refuge (indicated in white). In order to ensure that anyone needing to flee to one of these cities could arrive safely within a day or two, the cities were strategically located throughout the country. These specially designated cities reflect the high value placed on human life in ancient Israelite society. Life was so sacred that if someone was killed—even accidentally—the death needed to be atoned for by blood. Their "eye for an eye, tooth for a tooth" culture permitted a victim's next of kin to take the life of the perpetrator—even if the death was accidental. These cities, then, provided a necessary sanctuary for the person who accidentally killed another person. The person who fled here was required to remain in the city of refuge until the death of the high priest (Numbers 35:28).

The photograph on this page shows the landscapes of Kadesh, near the city of refuge for the northern area of Israel.

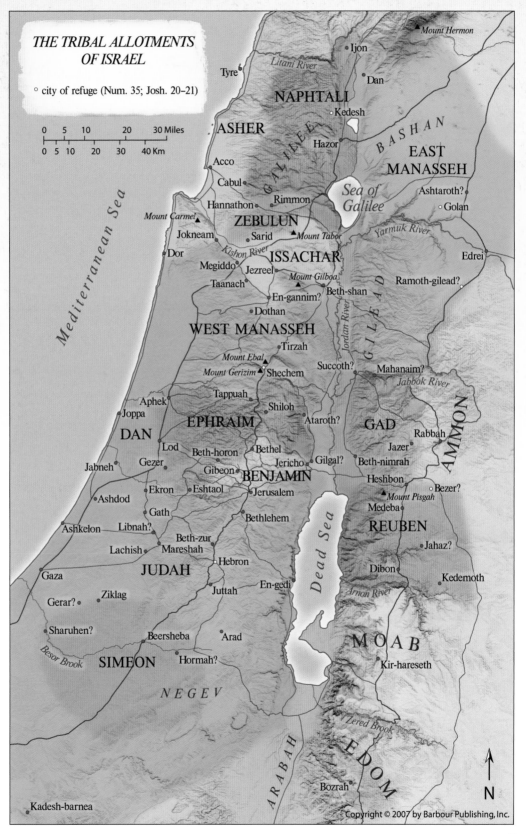

THE TRIBAL ALLOTMENTS
OF ISRAEL

○ city of refuge (Num. 35; Josh. 20–21)

0   5   10   20   30 Miles
0 5 10   20   30   40 Km

Mount Hermon

Ijon

Litani River

Tyre

Dan

NAPHTALI

Kedesh

ASHER

BASHAN

Hazor

EAST
MANASSEH

Acco

Sea of
Galilee

Ashtaroth?

Cabul

Golan

Hannathon

Rimmon

Mount Carmel

ZEBULUN

Yarmuk River

Jokneam

Sarid

Mount Tabor

Edrei

Kishon River

Dor

ISSACHAR

Megiddo

Jezreel

Mount Gilboa

Ramoth-gilead?

Taanach

Beth-shan

En-gannim?

Dothan

WEST MANASSEH

Tirzah

Mount Ebal

Succoth?

Mahanaim?

Mount Gerizim

Shechem

Jabbok River

Tappuah

Aphek

Shiloh

Joppa

EPHRAIM

Ataroth?

GAD

Rabbah

DAN

Lod

Bethel

Jazer

AMMON

Beth-horon

Jericho

Gilgal?

Beth-nimrah

Jabneh

Gezer

Gibeon

BENJAMIN

Heshbon

Bezer?

Ekron

Eshtaol

Jerusalem

Mount Pisgah

Ashdod

Medeba

Gath

Bethlehem

REUBEN

Ashkelon

Libnah?

Dead Sea

Lachish

Beth-zur

Mareshah

Hebron

Dibon

Jahaz?

Gaza

JUDAH

En-gedi

Kedemoth

Gerar?

Ziklag

Juttah

Arnon River

Sharuhen?

Beersheba

Arad

M O A B

Besor Brook

SIMEON

Hormah?

Kir-hareseth

N E G E V

Zered Brook

A R A B A H

E D O M

Kadesh-barnea

Bozrah

N

Mediterranean Sea

Jordan River

GILEAD

ISRAEL DURING THE TIME OF THE JUDGES

Before kings ruled over the Israelites, they were led by leaders known as judges. These judges were known for their military leadership and for being led by God's Spirit. These judges would rise up for a time to combat a particular foe, and then later another would arise somewhere else for another purpose.

In the previous generations, Moses and Joshua had instructed the Israelites to conquer or drive out all native peoples from the land. As the years went by, the Israelites left a number of cities unconquered (these cities are marked in white on the map). These remaining peoples created problems for the Israelites by leading them astray with idolatry and other sins—and occasionally fighting them on the battlefield. Judges often served to lead the Israelite army to break the hold of these and other invading enemies.

Below is a list of biblical judges.

Judge	Biblical Reference	The Enemy They Fought
Othniel	Judges 3:9–11	Mesopotamia
Ehud	Judges 3:15–30	Moabites
Shamgar	Judges 3:31	Philistines
Deborah and Barak	Judges 4:4–5:31	Canaanites
Gideon	Judges 6:7–8:35	Midianites
Tola	Judges 10:1–2	None listed
Jair	Judges 10:3–5	None listed
Jephthah	Judges 10:6–12:7	Ammonites
Ibzan	Judges 12:8–10	None listed
Elon	Judges 12:11–12	None listed
Abdon	Judges 12:13–15	None listed
Samson	Judges 13:2–16:31	Philistines
Eli	1 Samuel 1–4	None listed
Samuel	1 Samuel 7–9	Philistines

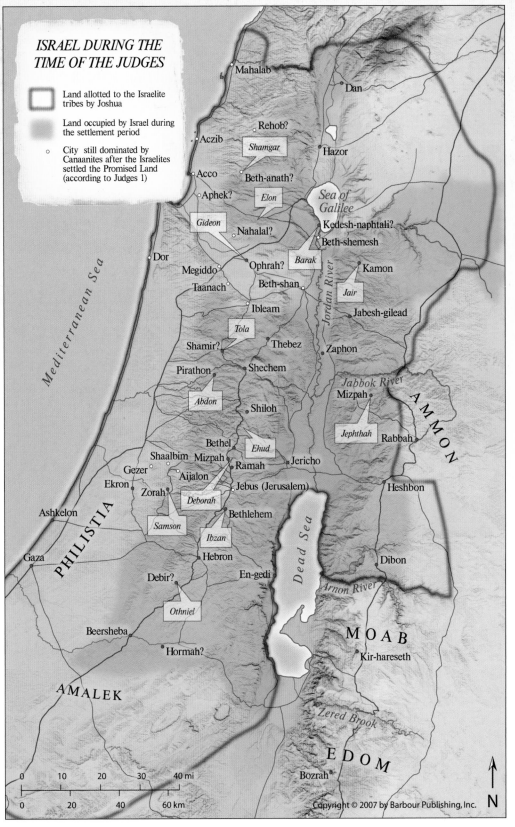

ISRAEL DURING THE TIME OF THE JUDGES

- Land allotted to the Israelite tribes by Joshua
- Land occupied by Israel during the settlement period
- City still dominated by Canaanites after the Israelites settled the Promised Land (according to Judges 1)

Mahalab

Dan

Rehob?

Aczib

Shamgar

Hazor

Acco

Beth-anath?

Aphek?

Elon

Sea of Galilee

Gideon

Nahalal?

Kedesh-naphtali?

Beth-shemesh

Dor

Ophrah?

Barak

Kamon

Megiddo

Beth-shan

Jair

Taanach

Jabesh-gilead

Ibleam

Tola

Shamir?

Thebez

Zaphon

Pirathon

Shechem

Jabbok River

Mizpah

AMMON

Abdon

Shiloh

Jephthah

Rabbah

Bethel

Ehud

Shaalbim

Mizpah

Jericho

Heshbon

Gezer

Ramah

Ekron

Aijalon

Jebus (Jerusalem)

Zorah

Deborah

Ashkelon

Bethlehem

Samson

Dead Sea

Ibzan

Gaza

Hebron

Dibon

PHILISTIA

Debir?

En-gedi

Arnon River

Othniel

Beersheba

MOAB

Hormah?

Kir-hareseth

AMALEK

Zered Brook

EDOM

Bozrah

Mediterranean Sea

Jordan River

| 0 | 10 | 20 | 30 | 40 mi |
| 0 | 20 | 40 | | 60 km |

Copyright © 2007 by Barbour Publishing, Inc.

N

DEBORAH AND BARAK DEFEAT THE CANAANITES

During the time of the judges, the Israelites repeatedly forgot the Lord and His promises in a regular cycle of sin, punishment, repentance and deliverance. First, the people abandoned God and sinned against Him. God then delivered them into the hands of their enemies. Eventually the people turned back to God, crying out for deliverance. Finally, God appointed a judge to lead them to victory over

their enemies. Soon afterward, however, the people turned away from God once more and the cycle began again.

During Deborah's time, Jabin, a king of Canaan, conquered the Israelites. When the people repented, God appointed Deborah (a prophetess of God and Israel's only female judge) and Barak (her military general) to lead the way. While Barak drew his army primarily from the nearby northern tribes of Zebulun and Naphtali, the battle force also included men from the tribes of Ephraim, Benjamin, and Manasseh. Barak's army assembled to confront the Canaanites at Mount Tabor (pictured on this page).

This mountain, a little more than ten miles from the Sea of Galilee, became the staging ground of the Israelites. With God's help, Barak and his army of ten thousand foot soldiers routed the chariot army of Jabin. (Read the story of the battle and Deborah's victory song in Judges 4–5.)

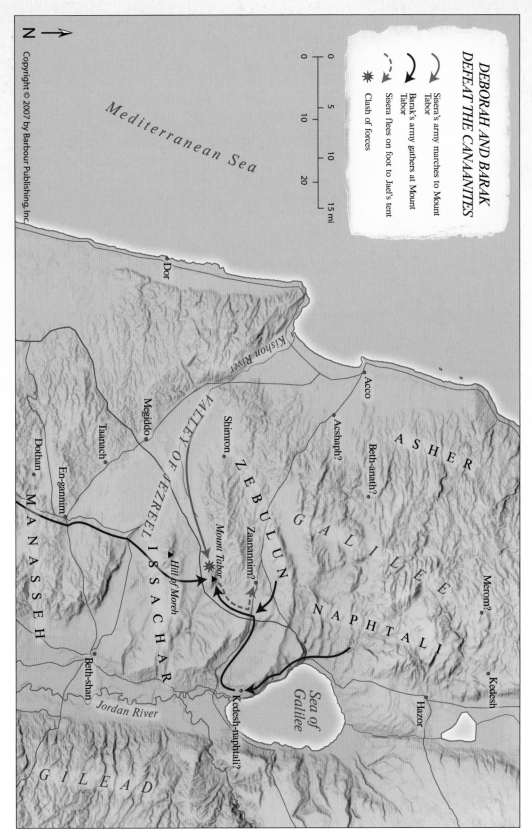

N

DEBORAH AND BARAK DEFEAT THE CANAANITES

Sisera's army marches to Mount Tabor

Barak's army gathers at Mount Tabor

Sisera flees on foot to Jael's tent

✳ Clash of forces

0 5 10 20

0 10 15 mi

Mediterranean Sea

Copyright © 2007 by Barbour Publishing, Inc.

Dor

Kishon River

Acco

Megiddo

Acshaph?

Beth-anath?

Taanach

Shimron

A S H E R

Dothan

Z E B U L U N

G A L I L E E

En-gannim

Mount Tabor

Zaanannim?

N A P H T A L I

Merom?

M A N A S S E H

I S S A C H A R

Hill of Moreh

VALLEY OF JEZREEL

Kedesh

Beth-shan

Kedesh-naphtali?

Hazor

Jordan River

Sea of Galilee

G I L E A D

45

GIDEON DEFEATS THE MIDIANITES

The story of Gideon opens with God's people beginning the predictable cycle found so often in Judges: "Again the Israelites did evil in the eyes of the LORD" (6:1). This time, God handed them over to serve the Midianites for seven years.

In anointing Gideon as Israel's next judge, God selected an unlikely hero. By Gideon's own account, he came from an insignificant family. In addition to his insignificant heritage, Gideon's own personality seemed to lack the confidence and assertiveness we would normally expect to find in a leader.

When Gideon finally accepted the mission and trusted God for the result, God put that trust to the test by reducing the size of Gideon's large army to a tiny force of three hundred men. At the Valley of Jezreel near the hill of Moreh (see photo), God, Gideon, and the small army used creative battle tactics to route the Midianite army and chase them deep into the Arabian Desert.

By using an unlikely hero and unlikely methods, God made sure He received the credit for routing another enemy from the land of Israel (Judges 6–8).

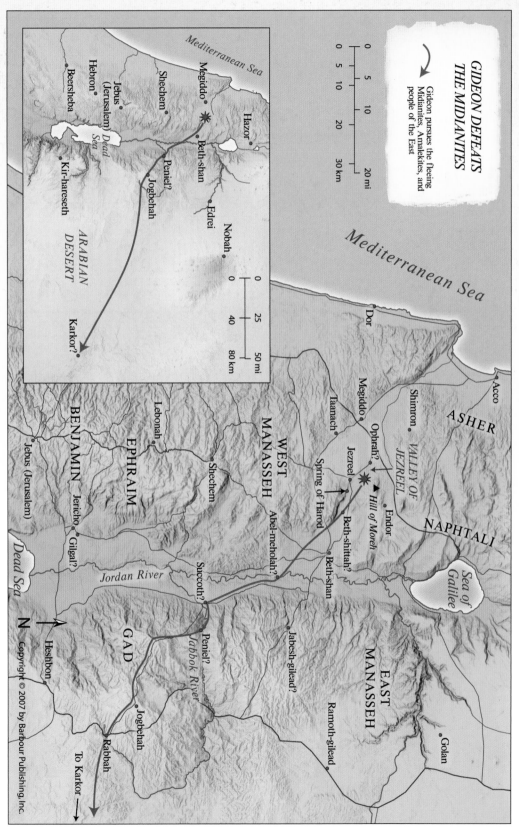

GIDEON DEFEATS
THE MIDIANITES

Gideon pursues the fleeing Midianites, Amalekites, and people of the East

JEPHTHAH DEFEATS THE AMMONITES

The people of Israel found themselves facing a familiar enemy when the Ammonites initiated a land dispute and moved westward to reclaim land they felt rightfully belonged to them. Hearing His people call for help, God selected another unlikely candidate for the job of judge—Jephthah, the son of a prostitute (Judges 11:1).

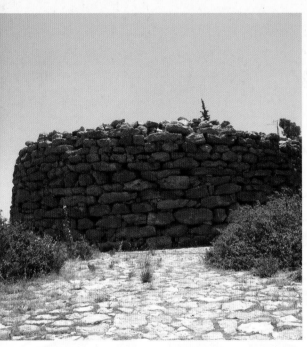

Jephthah, whose father was Gilead, grew into a strong man and a skilled soldier. However, since he lived in a culture where heritage mattered, Jephthah's stepbrothers drove him away and Jephthah settled in Tob.

After the Ammonites attacked the people of Israel, the elders began to search for the right leader to lead the military campaign against their enemies. Remembering Jephthah, the elders traveled to Tob, convinced him to take the leadership position, and brought him back to his people.

Filled with the Spirit of God, Jephthah led an attack, pushed south, and won victories against twenty cities. (During this series of battles Jephthah also made a reckless vow. See Judges 11:29–40 for details.) After winning an important and decisive battle, Jephthah was greeted not with cheers and accolades but with hostility from his fellow countrymen. Angry that they had not participated in the battle (and therefore missed out on its plunder), men from the tribe of Ephraim blamed Jephthah. Tensions escalated until war broke out at Zaphon, where Jephthah easily defeated his opponents. The story of the Ammonites' invasion and Jephthah can be read in Judges 10–12.

The photo on this page is of a tower built by the Ammonites.

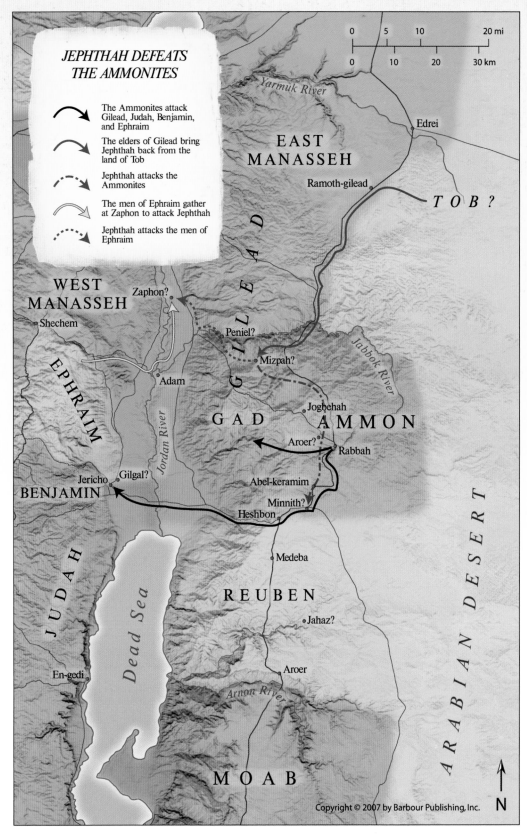

JEPHTHAH DEFEATS
THE AMMONITES

The Ammonites attack Gilead, Judah, Benjamin, and Ephraim

The elders of Gilead bring Jephthah back from the land of Tob

Jephthah attacks the Ammonites

The men of Ephraim gather at Zaphon to attack Jephthah

Jephthah attacks the men of Ephraim

Yarmuk River

Edrei

EAST MANASSEH

Ramoth-gilead

T O B ?

WEST MANASSEH

Zaphon?

Shechem

G I L E A D

Peniel?

Jabbok River

Mizpah?

EPHRAIM

Adam

Jogbehah

G A D

AMMON

Jordan River

Aroer?

Rabbah

Gilgal?

Jericho

Abel-keramim

BENJAMIN

Minnith?

Heshbon

Medeba

JUDAH

Dead Sea

R E U B E N

Jahaz?

En-gedi

Aroer

Arnon River

A R A B I A N   D E S E R T

M O A B

Copyright © 2007 by Barbour Publishing, Inc.

N

SAMSON'S DEEDS AND ISRAEL'S ATTACK OF GIBEAH

Somewhere between Zorah and Eshtaol lies the location of Samson's birth and burial. While the exact spot is unknown, this photograph highlights the traditional site of his tomb.

Samson's life and death were both characterized by self-imposed tragedy, beginning with an ill-advised decision to marry a Philistine woman. (His journey into the Philistine area is marked by red on the map.) Before his honeymoon ended, Samson traveled to Ashkelon where he killed and plundered thirty Philistines to pay off a wager made during his wedding feast. When Samson returned to reconcile his debt, he learned that his new wife had been given in marriage to someone else (Judges 14). In revenge, he destroyed a large portion of the Philistine crops. Before the Philistines could exact punishment, Samson single-handedly killed one thousand of them with the jawbone of a donkey at Lehi (Judges 15).

Later, he visited the heart of the Philistine country in Gaza and spent the night with a prostitute. When the men of Gaza prepared to capture him, Samson escaped by ripping out the city gates, which he carried to the Israelite city of Hebron (as indicated by the dotted red lines and found in Judges 16).

Betrayed by Delilah and finally captured by the Philistines, Samson refocused his heart on God. He used his great strength to push down the building where he was held prisoner—killing himself as well as his Philistine captors.

While God used Samson to break the Philistines' hold over Israel, God was also concerned enough with the spiritual state of His people to discipline them as necessary. The blue and yellow lines recount a gruesome story from Judges 20 involving the Benjamites; when they had sinned, the remaining tribes of Israel inflicted a harsh punishment on their brothers. These stories illustrate how the days of the judges were marked by darkness and violence.

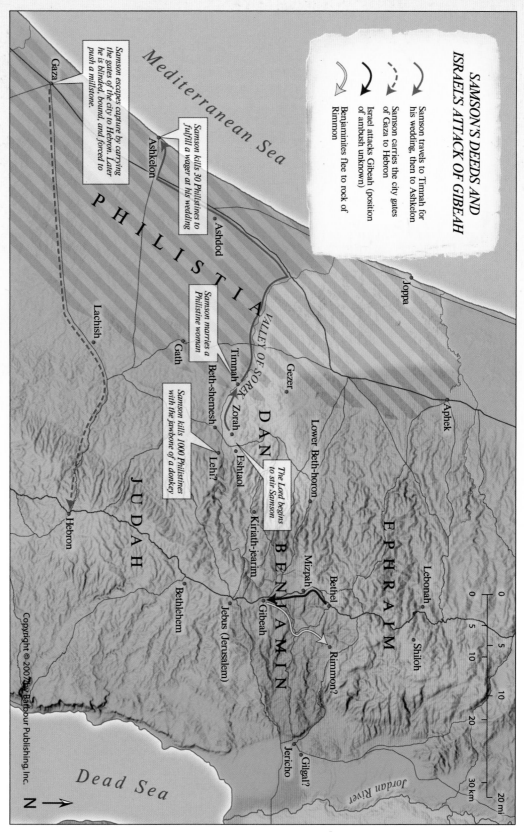

SAMSON'S DEEDS AND
ISRAEL'S ATTACK OF GIBEAH

Samson travels to Timnah for
his wedding, then to Ashkelon

Samson carries the city gates
of Gaza to Hebron

Israel attacks Gibeah (position
of ambush unknown)

Benjaminites flee to rock of
Rimmon

Samson escapes capture by carrying
the gates of the city to Hebron. Later
he is blinded, bound, and forced to
push a millstone.

Samson kills 30 Philistines to
fulfill a wager at his wedding

Samson marries a
Philistine woman

Samson kills 1000 Philistines
with the jawbone of a donkey

The Lord begins
to stir Samson

Mediterranean Sea

P H I L I S T I A

Gaza

Ashkelon

Ashdod

Joppa

Lachish

Gath

Beth-shemesh

Timnah

Zorah

Lehi?

Eshtaol

Kiriath-jearim

Gezer

VALLEY OF SOREK

Lower Beth-horon

D A N

J U D A H

B E N J A M I N

E P H R A I M

Hebron

Bethlehem

Jebus (Jerusalem)

Gibeah

Mizpah

Bethel

Rimmon?

Lebonah

Shiloh

Aphek

Gilgal?

Jericho

Dead Sea

Jordan River

N →

0   5   10   20   30 km
0   5   10   20 mi

THE ARK OF THE COVENANT IS CAPTURED AND RETURNED

God had commissioned the Ark of the Covenant (see photo of replica) as a tangible reminder of His power and presence. Designed to induce awe and respect, the ark was most often kept in the tabernacle—the center of Israelite worship.

During the days of Eli the priest, the Israelites experienced military defeat against the Philistines (1 Samuel 4). Desperately looking for a way to secure victory, Eli's sons led the Israelites into battle while carrying the Ark of the Covenant as a lucky charm.

God's presence, however, depended not upon the Ark of the Covenant but upon the God of the covenant—and the Israelites' attempt to secure a victory apart from faithfulness to the covenant failed. Eli's sons were killed at Ebenezer, and the Philistines captured the ark, putting the sacred box in the temple of Dagon. To their dismay, every place the Philistines brought the ark, God demonstrated His power by bringing them misfortune (1 Samuel 5). Finally, in an effort to rid themselves of the terrible plagues, the Philistines put the ark on a cart and sent the oxen back within Israel's borders (1 Samuel 6).

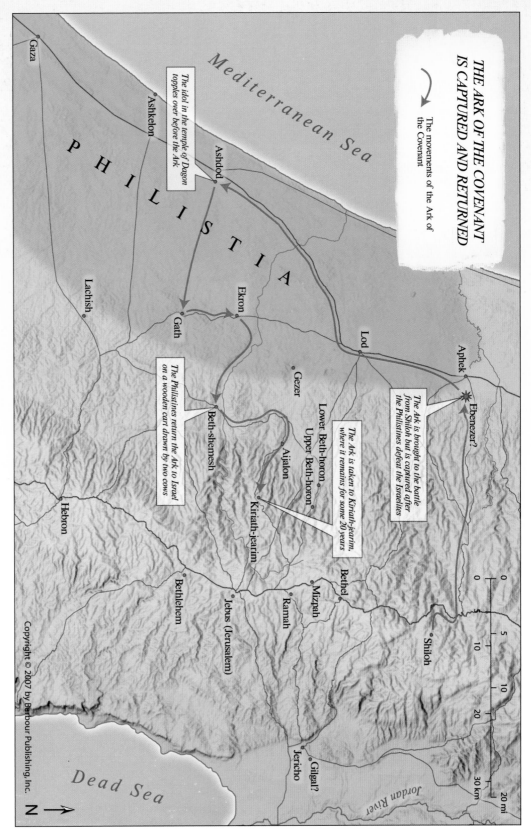

THE ARK OF THE COVENANT
IS CAPTURED AND RETURNED

The movements of the Ark of
the Covenant

Mediterranean Sea

PHILISTIA

Gaza

Ashkelon

Ashdod

The idol in the temple of Dagon
topples over before the Ark

Lachish

Ekron

Gath

Gezer

Lod

Aphek

Ebenezer?

The Ark is brought to the battle
from Shiloh but is captured after
the Philistines defeat the Israelites

Lower Beth-horon
Upper Beth-horon

The Ark is taken to Kiriath-jearim,
where it remains for some 20 years

The Philistines return the Ark to Israel
on a wooden cart drawn by two cows

Beth-shemesh

Aijalon

Kiriath-jearim

Hebron

Bethlehem

Jebus (Jerusalem)

Ramah

Mizpah

Bethel

Shiloh

Jericho

Gilgal?

Jordan River

Dead Sea

N →

0
0
5
5
10
10
20
30 km
20 mi

ISRAEL DURING THE TIME OF SAUL

The events at the beginning of Saul's reign helped Saul solidify his leadership: Though Samuel had already anointed him as king (1 Samuel 10), Saul had not assumed kingship with a grandiose display of power. Instead of acting as Israel's new leader, Saul returned to his home and was plowing his fields when the Ammonites attacked Jabesh Gilead (1 Samuel 11). Saul left his fields, mustered 330,000 men at Bezek, and easily defeated the enemy at Jabesh Gilead. The people celebrated the event by renewing Saul's kingship at Gilgal.

Later, Saul and his son Jonathan won a decisive battle against the Philistines. The turning point for the battle came at Michmash, where "Jonathan climbed up, using his hands and feet, with his

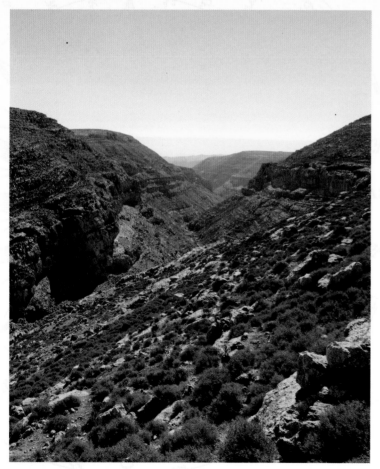

armor-bearer right behind him. The Philistines fell before Jonathan, and his armor-bearer followed and killed behind him" (1 Samuel 14:13). Jonathan's remarkable victory over the Philistine outpost occurred near these rough cliffs (see photo and inset map). On this rocky crag, the prince and his armor-bearer climbed difficult terrain to lead the Israelite army to a surprising victory (read the story in 1 Samuel 14).

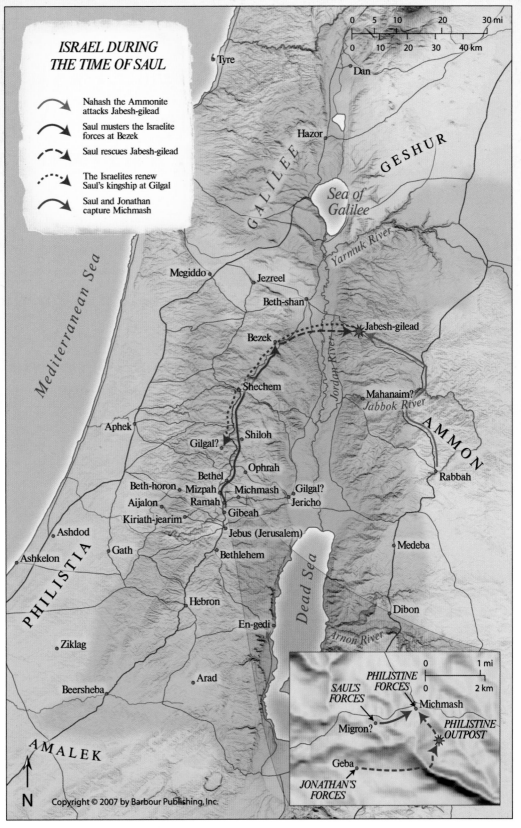

ISRAEL DURING THE TIME OF SAUL

Nahash the Ammonite attacks Jabesh-gilead

Saul musters the Israelite forces at Bezek

Saul rescues Jabesh-gilead

The Israelites renew Saul's kingship at Gilgal

Saul and Jonathan capture Michmash

Copyright © 2007 by Barbour Publishing, Inc.

DAVID AND SAUL: FROM GIBEAH TO THE STRONGHOLD

David's military success (see inset and 1 Samuel 17–18) and popularity with the people ended up forcing him to spend many years on the lam running from a jealous King Saul. Rather than fight the king directly and risk harming God's anointed

leader, David evaded him by moving from place to place. However, God used this time to prepare David for his future career as king and commander-in-chief of the Israelite army. The map to the right highlights eight stops David made as he moved to avoid confrontation with Saul.

Location	Biblical Reference	Key Event
Gibeah	1 Samuel 19:11	David is rescued by his wife Michal (the daughter of Saul).
Ramah	1 Samuel 19:18	David meets with the prophet Samuel.
Gibeah	1 Samuel 20:42	Jonathan (the son of Saul) warns David of trouble.
Nob	1 Samuel 21:1	The priest gives David the sword of Goliath.
Gath	1 Samuel 21:10	David escapes harm by pretending to be insane.
Adullam	1 Samuel 22:1	David gathers 400 men (see photo of location).
Mizpah	1 Samuel 22:3–4	David places his parents in the care of the king of Moab.
The Stronghold	1 Samuel 22:4	David waits for God's instruction.

DAVID DEFEATS GOLIATH

VALLEY OF SOREK

VALLEY OF ELAH

ISRAELITE CAMP

David kills the Philistine champion Goliath with a stone from a sling

The Israelites pursue the fleeing Philistines as far as Gath and Ekron

PHILISTINE CAMP

Ekron · Timnah · Zorah · Beth-shemesh · Gath · Azekah · Socoh · Adullam

PHILISTIA

Bethel · Mizpah · Gilgal? · Jericho · Lower Beth-horon · Upper Beth-horon · Ramah · Gibeah · Nob · Gezer · Kiriath-jearim · Ekron · Beth-shemesh · Jebus (Jerusalem) · Bethlehem · Heshbon

The priest gives David the sword of Goliath

David's birthplace and childhood home

Gath · Adullam · Keilah · Lachish · FOREST OF HERETH? · Hebron · Ziph · Carmel · Maon · En-gedi · Dead Sea · Dibon

David pretends to be insane

David gathers an army of about 400 men

The Stronghold? (Masada)

Arad · Beersheba

MOAB

Mizpeh of Moab? (Kir-hareseth)

David places his parents in the care of the king of Moab

AMALEK

DAVID AND SAUL: FROM GIBEAH TO THE STRONGHOLD

① Places where David stops as he flees from Saul

Zoar

N

Copyright © 2007 by Barbour Publishing, Inc.

57

DAVID AND SAUL: FROM THE STRONG-HOLD TO ZIKLAG

David's flight from Saul lasted many years. Below are additional places David sought refuge.

Location	Biblical Reference	Key Event
The Stronghold	1 Samuel 22:4	David waits for God's instruction.
Forest of Hereth	1 Samuel 22:5	The prophet Gad sends David to hide here.
Keilah	1 Samuel 23:1–2	David rescues Keilah from the Philistine invaders.
Ziph	1 Samuel 23:14–24	David meets Jonathan and then is betrayed by the men of Ziph.
Desert of Maon	1 Samuel 23:25	David narrowly escapes capture when Saul cuts off pursuit because of the invading Philistine army.
En-Gedi	1 Samuel 24:1	David resists the opportunity to kill Saul while resting in a cave (see photo of En Gedi caves).
The Stronghold	1 Samuel 24:22	David rests here after pledging new allegiance to Saul.
Desert of Maon	1 Samuel 25–26	Nabal insults David. David meets Abigail and turns down a second chance to kill Saul.
Gath	1 Samuel 27:2	David seeks asylum with Achish.
Ziklag	1 Samuel 27:6	Achish gives David a home in the city of Ziklag.

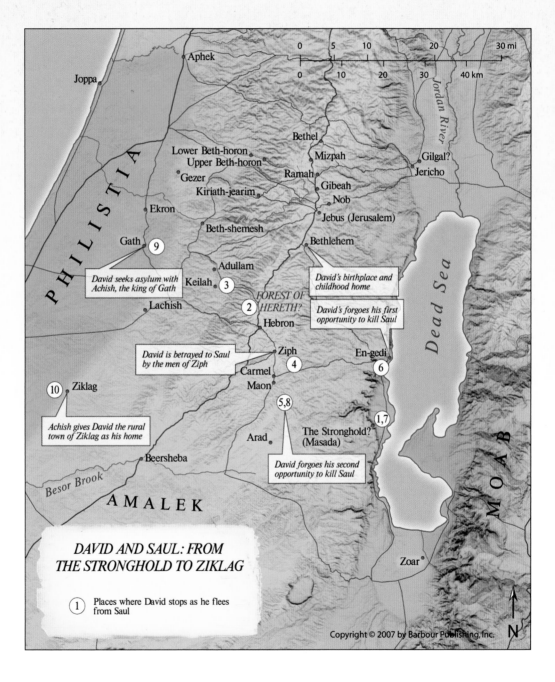

DAVID AND SAUL: FROM
THE STRONGHOLD TO ZIKLAG

① Places where David stops as he flees
from Saul

Copyright © 2007 by Barbour Publishing, Inc.

DAVID PURSUES THE AMALEKITES

While David lived in Philistine territory, he feigned loyalty to their king and fabricated stories about how he had harmed the people of Judah (1 Samuel 27). When the Philistines marched north to attack Saul at Aphek, David even followed in an apparent act of solidarity. After the other commanders expressed their distrust that David would fight his own countrymen, King Achish sent David home.

Once David and his army of six hundred men arrived back at Ziklag (see photo of location), they discovered that the Amalekites had attacked the city and carried off all the remaining residents as captives. (The Amalekites had hassled Israel in previous generations. See Exodus 17 and Judges 6.)

David pursued the Amalekite raiding party, defeated them, and brought everyone back home safely. Rather than keeping the plunder they obtained from the Amalekites, David built goodwill by sending gifts to a number of cities across the southern part of Israel. (Read the story in 1 Samuel 30.)

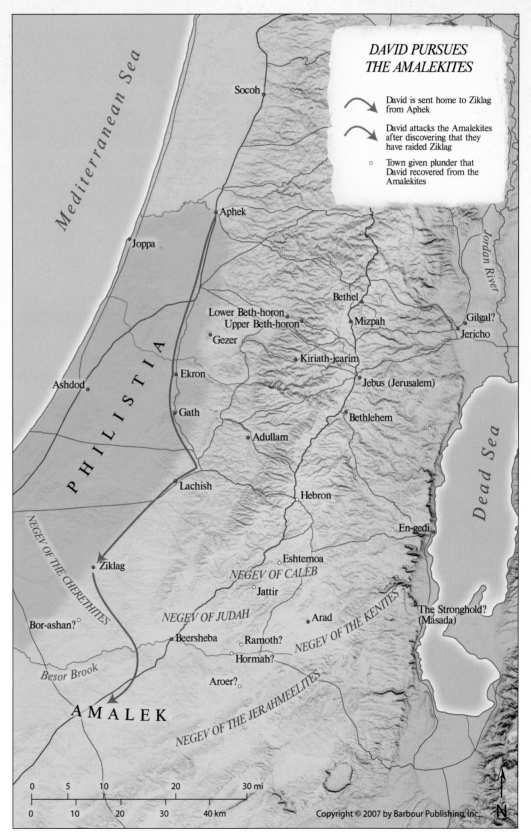

DAVID PURSUES THE AMALEKITES

David is sent home to Ziklag from Aphek

David attacks the Amalekites after discovering that they have raided Ziklag

○ Town given plunder that David recovered from the Amalekites

Mediterranean Sea

Socoh

Aphek

Joppa

Jordan River

Bethel

Lower Beth-horon
Upper Beth-horon

Mizpah

Gilgal?

Jericho

Gezer

Kiriath-jearim

Ekron

Jebus (Jerusalem)

Ashdod

Gath

Bethlehem

P H I L I S T I A

Adullam

Lachish

Hebron

Dead Sea

NEGEV OF THE CHERETHITES

En-gedi

Eshtemoa

NEGEV OF CALEB

Ziklag

Jattir

The Stronghold?
(Masada)

NEGEV OF THE KENITES

NEGEV OF JUDAH

Arad

Bor-ashan?○

Beersheba

Ramoth?○

Hormah?○

Besor Brook

Aroer?○

NEGEV OF THE JERAHMEELITES

A M A L E K

| 0 | 5 | 10 | 20 | 30 mi |
| 0 | 10 | 20 | 30 | 40 km |

Copyright © 2007 by Barbour Publishing, Inc.

N

THE BATTLE AT MOUNT GILBOA

Apparently King Saul sensed that God's blessing had left him and that the looming battle against the Philistines would end in disaster. With the army assembled in Jezreel, Saul secretly met with the witch of Endor in an effort to communicate with Samuel through an ancient séance. Saul indeed saw a vision of Samuel, which only confirmed his fear of imminent doom (1 Samuel 28).

At the beginning of the battle, the Philistines drove the Israelites south to Mt. Gilboa (see photo). With their backs against the mountain, Saul and his son Jonathan died (1 Samuel 31).

When Saul first became king, he solidified his leadership by rescuing the town of Jabesh-gilead from an invading army (see page 55). Now, at the end of his life, the people of this town honored their late king and his sons by traveling through the night to rescue their abused bodies and honorably cremate their remains.

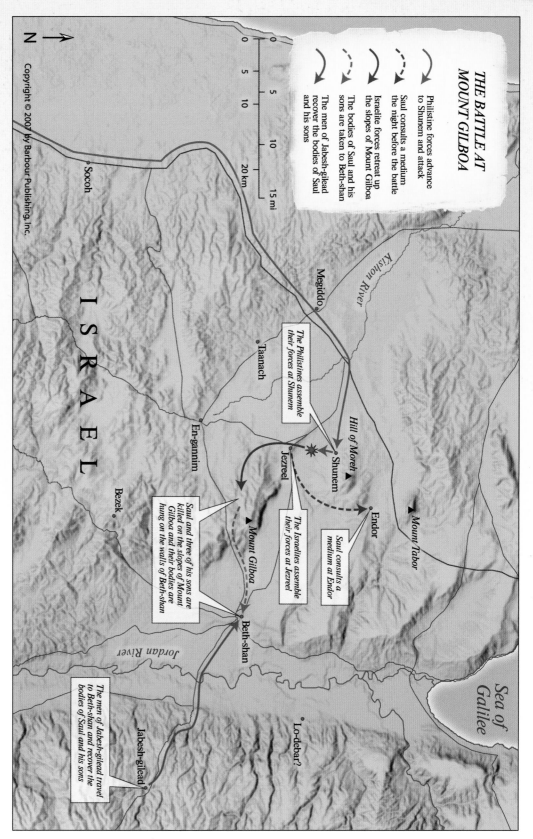

THE BATTLE AT
MOUNT GILBOA

Philistine forces advance
to Shunem and attack

Saul consults a medium
the night before the battle

Israelite forces retreat up
the slopes of Mount Gilboa

The bodies of Saul and his
sons are taken to Beth-shan

The men of Jabesh-gilead
recover the bodies of Saul
and his sons

N

0   5   10   20 km

0   5   10   15 mi

Socoh

I S R A E L

Megiddo

Kishon River

Taanach

En-gannim

Bezek

The Philistines assemble
their forces at Shunem

Hill of Moreh

Shunem

Jezreel

Endor

Mount Tabor

Mount Gilboa

Saul and three of his sons are
killed on the slopes of Mount
Gilboa and their bodies are
hung on the walls of Beth-shan

The Israelites assemble
their forces at Jezreel

Saul consults a
medium at Endor

Beth-shan

Jordan River

Lo-debar?

Sea of
Galilee

Jabesh-gilead

The men of Jabesh-gilead travel
to Beth-shan and recover the
bodies of Saul and his sons

63

DAVID SECURES HIS REIGN OVER ISRAEL

The transition from Saul's kingship to David's reign was neither simple nor swift. Following typical rules of succession, the people first appointed Saul's son Ish-bosheth as king (2 Samuel 2:10). Only the tribe of Judah looked to David as their new king.

For two years, civil war existed between David and his army (led by Joab) and Ish-bosheth and his army (led by Abner). The conflict was highlighted by a bloody battle at the pool of Gibeon (see photograph of this location above, and read the story in 2 Samuel 2).

The war came to an end quickly when conflict arose between Ish-bosheth and Abner. After an internal power struggle, Abner defected and pledged his allegiance to David (2 Samuel 3). With Ish-bosheth's primary protector gone, the son of Saul was assassinated—having reigned for two years.

Rather than look to another member of Saul's house to lead them, the people of Israel finally united under David and pledged allegiance to their new king (2 Samuel 5).

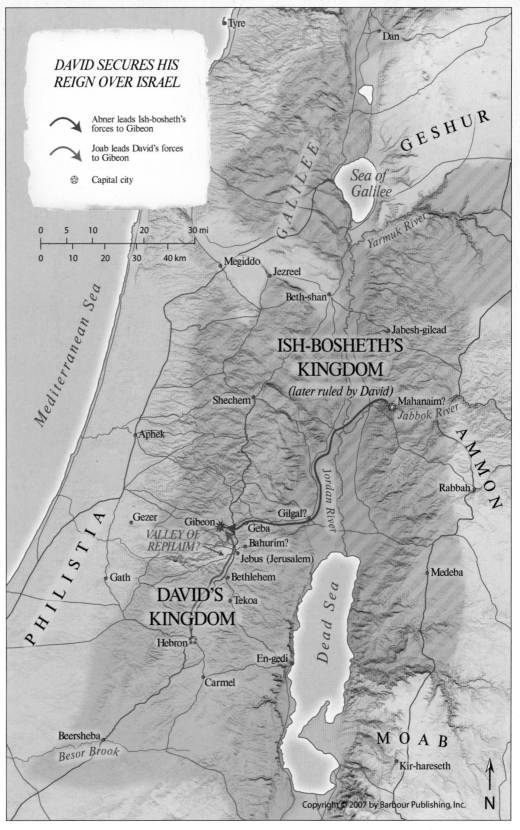

DAVID SECURES HIS REIGN OVER ISRAEL

Abner leads Ish-bosheth's forces to Gibeon

Joab leads David's forces to Gibeon

Capital city

Tyre

Dan

GESHUR

GALILEE

Sea of Galilee

Yarmuk River

Megiddo

Jezreel

Beth-shan

Jabesh-gilead

ISH-BOSHETH'S KINGDOM
(later ruled by David)

Mahanaim?
Jabbok River

AMMON

Shechem

Aphek

Jordan River

Rabbah

Mediterranean Sea

Gezer

Gibeon

Gilgal?

Geba

VALLEY OF REPHAIM?

Bahurim?

Jebus (Jerusalem)

Medeba

Gath

Bethlehem

DAVID'S KINGDOM

Tekoa

Dead Sea

Hebron

En-gedi

Carmel

Beersheba

Besor Brook

MOAB

Kir-hareseth

N

DAVID DEFEATS THE AMMONITES AND THE ARAMEANS

David's reign as king began with a series of military victories (see 2 Samuel 5, 8). In these conflicts, David defeated hostile neighbors to the west (the Philistines) and to the southeast (the Moabites). The Ammonites, his neighbors to the east, faced the choice of living peacefully with their neighbors or going to war with them.

When the king of Ammon died, David sent an envoy to express condolences to the new king. Rather than accept these men peacefully, the new king (Hanun) suspected the men of espionage. He treated them harshly, shaving half their beards and tearing their garments. These humiliated men stayed at Jericho until their beards grew back (2 Samuel 10).

When the Ammonites realized that war was imminent, they hired twenty thousand Aramean soldiers to help join the battle against David. Their effort to open a second front failed as David and his military commanders routed their enemies and subdued their neighbors to the east.

The photo shows the remains of a fort near Medeba that would have been in use around the time of this battle.

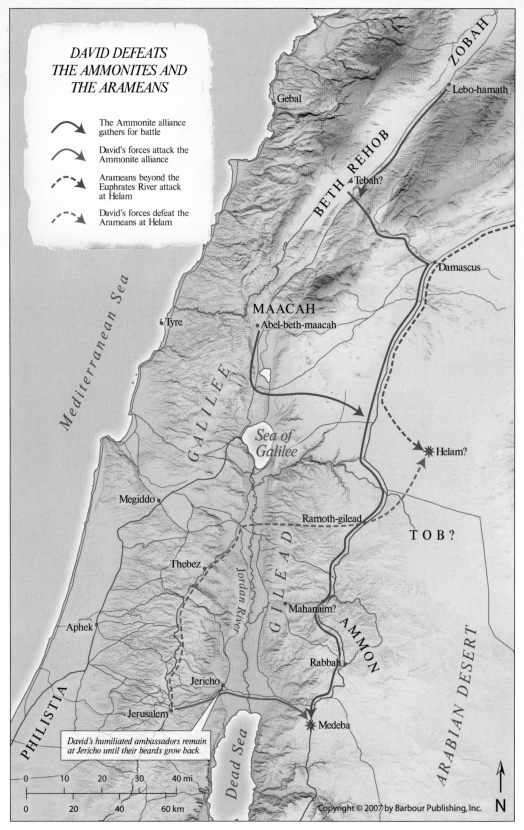

DAVID DEFEATS
THE AMMONITES AND
THE ARAMEANS

The Ammonite alliance
gathers for battle

David's forces attack the
Ammonite alliance

Arameans beyond the
Euphrates River attack
at Helam

David's forces defeat the
Arameans at Helam

ZOBAH

Lebo-hamath

Gebal

BETH REHOB

Tebah?

Damascus

Mediterranean Sea

Tyre

MAACAH

Abel-beth-maacah

GALILEE

Sea of
Galilee

Helam?

Megiddo

Ramoth-gilead

TOB ?

Thebez

Jordan River

GILEAD

Mahanaim?

Aphek

AMMON

Rabbah

ARABIAN DESERT

Jericho

PHILISTIA

Jerusalem

David's humiliated ambassadors remain
at Jericho until their beards grow back

Medeba

Dead Sea

0   10   20   30   40 mi

0   20   40   60 km

Copyright © 2007 by Barbour Publishing, Inc.

N

THE EXTENT OF DAVID'S KINGDOM

When Saul began his reign, the kingdom was a loose confederation of tribes rather than a well-organized, nationalistic kingdom. Over time, the monarchy's authority became more centralized and additional territory was added to the kingdom.

When David became king (2 Samuel 5), he made Jerusalem the new capital city. This "City of David" became both the civil and religious capital of the land. Remains of David's fortress have recently been found and are currently being excavated (see photo of the work in progress).

With a growing organization and structure to his government and military, David defeated the Philistines, Moabites, Ammonites, Arameans, and Edomites. As the population of Israel grew, David secured and expanded Israel's borders. This resulted in a country whose boundaries more closely matched God's promises given through Moses and Joshua.

Solomon became king and continued to organize the country of Israel. He used a conscripted labor force to complete magnificent building projects, accumulated vast wealth through domination of the trade routes, and ruled through a peaceful time (1 Kings 4:24). By historical accounts, the kingdom of Israel was more powerful and better organized than the surrounding peoples of this era, allowing its boundaries to continue to grow during a fairly peaceful time.

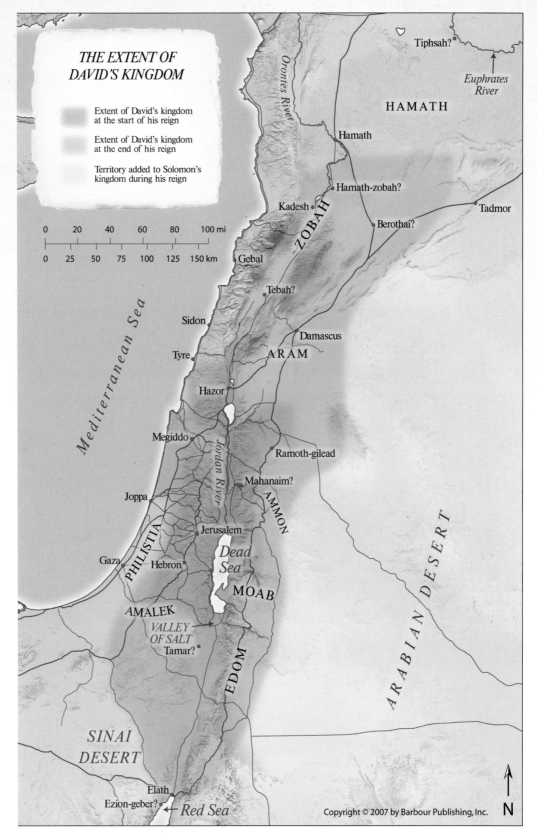

THE EXTENT OF DAVID'S KINGDOM

Extent of David's kingdom at the start of his reign

Extent of David's kingdom at the end of his reign

Territory added to Solomon's kingdom during his reign

```
0    20    40    60    80    100 mi
0   25   50   75  100  125  150 km
```

Tiphsah?

Euphrates River

Orontes River

HAMATH

Hamath

Hamath-zobah?

Kadesh

ZOBAH

Berothai?

Tadmor

Gebal

Tebah?

Sidon

Damascus

Tyre

ARAM

Hazor

Megiddo

Jordan River

Ramoth-gilead

Mahanaim?

Joppa

AMMON

PHILISTIA

Jerusalem

Gaza

Hebron

Dead Sea

MOAB

AMALEK

VALLEY OF SALT

Tamar?

EDOM

ARABIAN DESERT

Mediterranean Sea

SINAI DESERT

Elath

Ezion-geber?

Red Sea

N

ABSALOM'S REBELLION

Though often remembered for his many strengths, David was also a man with many weaknesses. The disarray of his family gave evidence of this. When his son Amnon raped his own half-sister, Tamar, David failed to address it. So his son Absalom took matters in his own hands and killed his step-brother Amnon. Absalom then fled to Geshur (see photo of what may have been the capital of this region). He stayed in this area with his mother's family while living in exile.

After three years, David's general, Joab, recruited a woman to manipulate the king into lifting the prince's banishment. After Absalom returned to Jerusalem, David extended his forgiveness (2 Samuel 14). Rather than being grateful for this welcome, Absalom worked at stealing away the hearts of the people and eventually set himself up as king in Hebron—the former seat of David's throne. This location made a symbolic statement while also providing a practical location for rallying support.

Upon hearing of Absalom's ambitions and growing support, David fled from Jerusalem. The armies of both men finally clashed in the Forest of Ephraim, resulting in Absalom's death and David's return to Jerusalem. (The full story of Absalom and his rebellion can be found in 2 Samuel 13–18.)

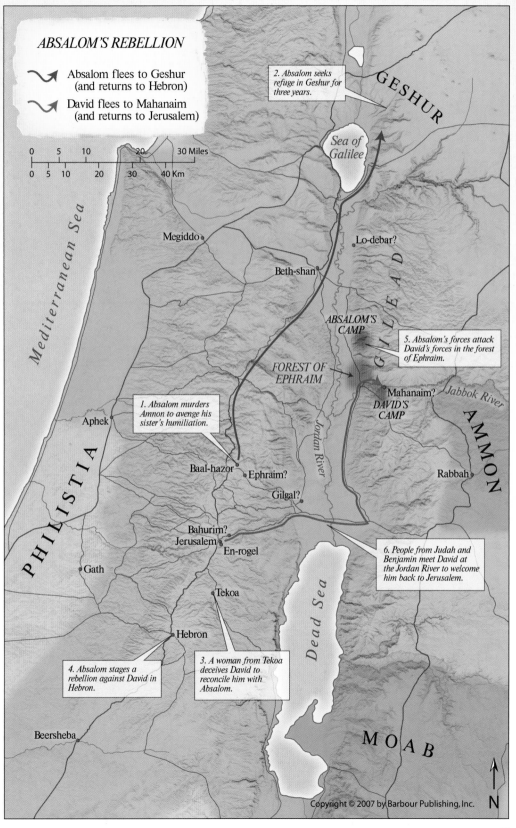

ABSALOM'S REBELLION

Absalom flees to Geshur
(and returns to Hebron)

David flees to Mahanaim
(and returns to Jerusalem)

0   5   10   20   30 Miles
0   5   10   20   30   40 Km

Mediterranean Sea

GESHUR

Sea of Galilee

Megiddo

Lo-debar?

Beth-shan

GILEAD

ABSALOM'S CAMP

FOREST OF EPHRAIM

Mahanaim?   *Jabbok River*

DAVID'S CAMP

AMMON

Aphek

Baal-hazor   Ephraim?

Jordan River

Gilgal?

Rabbah

Bahurim?
Jerusalem   En-rogel

PHILISTIA

Gath

Tekoa

Dead Sea

Hebron

Beersheba

M O A B

2. Absalom seeks refuge in Geshur for three years.

5. Absalom's forces attack David's forces in the forest of Ephraim.

1. Absalom murders Amnon to avenge his sister's humiliation.

6. People from Judah and Benjamin meet David at the Jordan River to welcome him back to Jerusalem.

4. Absalom stages a rebellion against David in Hebron.

3. A woman from Tekoa deceives David to reconcile him with Absalom.

N

JERUSALEM DURING SOLOMON'S TIME

A place of great importance to many, the Temple Mount is considered a holy site by members of the Jewish, Christian, and Muslim faiths. Such strong interest often results in political and religious conflict. Currently, the Temple Mount is under Islamic control.

This photograph, taken from the east, shows some ancient walls—built sometime after Solomon—as they exist today. (These are also noted on the map). The walls pictured were more expansive than the walls and city of Solomon's day. During the time of Solomon's reign, the city was smaller and simpler, but was certainly an adequate hub for social, commercial, and religious activity in ancient Israel.

The temple and home of Solomon were known to be glorious structures. The description of their sizes and some of their ornamentation can be found in 1 Kings 5–8.

SOLOMON'S
ADMINISTRATIVE
DISTRICTS

□ Building project of Solomon

① Administrative district of Solomon

Route of shipments for building the temple of the Lord

Solomon's son-in-law Ahimaaz is governor of the region of Naphtali

Solomon's son-in-law Ben-abinadab is governor of the region of Dor

Judah, Solomon's tribe, was exempt from the annual tax that provided for the king's needs

Sidon
Tyre
Dan
Hazor ⑧
ARAM
GESHUR
ARGOB?
Cabul
⑨
Sea of Galilee
⑩
Dor ④
Megiddo
Jezreel
Taanach
Beth-shan
GILEAD
⑥
Ramoth-gilead
Mediterranean Sea
HEPHER?
③
Socoh
⑤
Abel-meholah
Jordan River
Mahanaim?
AMMON
Shechem
Zarethan
Joppa
① Shiloh
⑦
Rabbah
Lower Beth-horon
Gezer Shaalbim
⑪
Baalath
② Jerusalem
Beth-shemesh
PHILISTIA
JUDAH
Dead Sea
⑫
Gaza
Hebron
Dibon
Beersheba
MOAB
Kir-hareseth
NEGEV
0 10 20 30 40 mi
0 20 40 60 km
Tamar?
N

Copyright © 2007 by Barbour Publishing, Inc.

SOLOMON'S INTERNATIONAL VENTURES

In addition to bringing peace, security, and building projects to the Holy Land, Solomon also brought economic prosperity. In fact, he accumulated so much gold that silver had little value (1 Kings 10:27; 2 Chronicles 9:20).

One of the ways Solomon increased the wealth of the country was through increasing the import and export business. For example, he purchased horses from Kue and Egypt to sell to the Hittites and Arameans (1 Kings 10:29). In addition to trading with his neighbors, Solomon built merchant ships that expanded commerce. First Kings 9:26 records information about the fleet that Solomon built on the Red Sea, which also contributed to trade efforts (see lines in red). In addition to these, he had other ships that returned "every three years. . .carrying gold, silver and ivory, and apes and baboons" (2 Chronicles 9:21). Israel's economy also grew and prospered by virtue of the country's location. As a centrally located, peaceful land, Israel became a natural trade route for merchants from all surrounding countries.

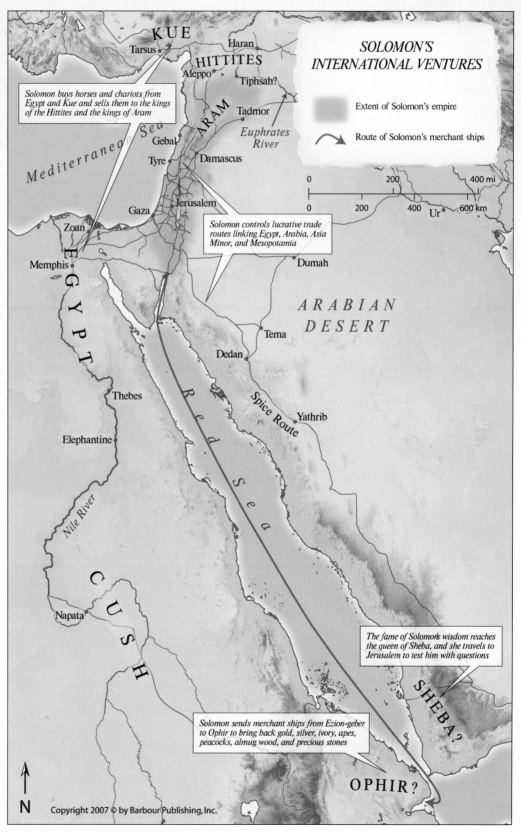

SOLOMON'S
INTERNATIONAL VENTURES

Extent of Solomon's empire

Route of Solomon's merchant ships

KUE

Tarsus

Haran

HITTITES

Aleppo

Tiphsah?

ARAM

Tadmor

Euphrates
River

Gebal

Tyre

Damascus

Mediterranean Sea

Solomon buys horses and chariots from
Egypt and Kue and sells them to the kings
of the Hittites and the kings of Aram

Gaza

Jerusalem

Zoan

Solomon controls lucrative trade
routes linking Egypt, Arabia, Asia
Minor, and Mesopotamia

Memphis

Dumah

Ur

EGYPT

ARABIAN
DESERT

Tema

Dedan

Thebes

Spice Route

Yathrib

Elephantine

Red Sea

Nile River

C U S H

Napata

The fame of Solomon's wisdom reaches
the queen of Sheba, and she travels to
Jerusalem to test him with questions

SHEBA?

Solomon sends merchant ships from Ezion-geber
to Ophir to bring back gold, silver, ivory, apes,
peacocks, almug wood, and precious stones

OPHIR?

N

Copyright 2007 © by Barbour Publishing, Inc.

77

THE KINGDOM DIVIDES

After Solomon's death, Israel divided into two kingdoms: the Northern Kingdom and the Southern Kingdom. The ten tribes of the north rebelled against King Rehoboam, seceded from the kingdom, and established Jeroboam as the king of the "new" Israel. In the south, the tribe of Judah remained loyal to King Rehoboam and the Davidic line and became known as the nation of Judah.

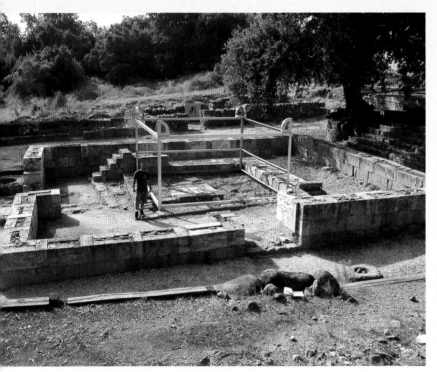

Since the Southern Kingdom controlled the temple, King Jeroboam of the Northern Kingdom feared his people would defect when they traveled to Jerusalem to worship: "Jeroboam thought to himself, 'The kingdom will now likely revert to the house of David. If these people go up to offer sacrifices at the temple of the LORD in Jerusalem, they will again give their allegiance to their lord, Rehoboam king of Judah. They will kill me and return to King Rehoboam' " (1 Kings 12:26–27).

To avoid this end, King Jeroboam set up idols at Bethel and Dan (see map). These conveniently-located cities sat on the northern and southern ends of the kingdom and became centers of worship for the people living in the Northern Kingdom. The photograph shows the actual site of the high place in the northern city of Dan. The reconstructed metal frame shows the probable location and size of the original altar built by Jeroboam.

Soon after the kingdom divided, King Shishak of Egypt raided the cities of Judah and Israel, carrying off significant treasures and wealth. The biblical account includes references to the attacks against Judah's cities, and archaeological evidence reveals that the attacks also included some of Israel's northern cities (2 Chronicles 12).

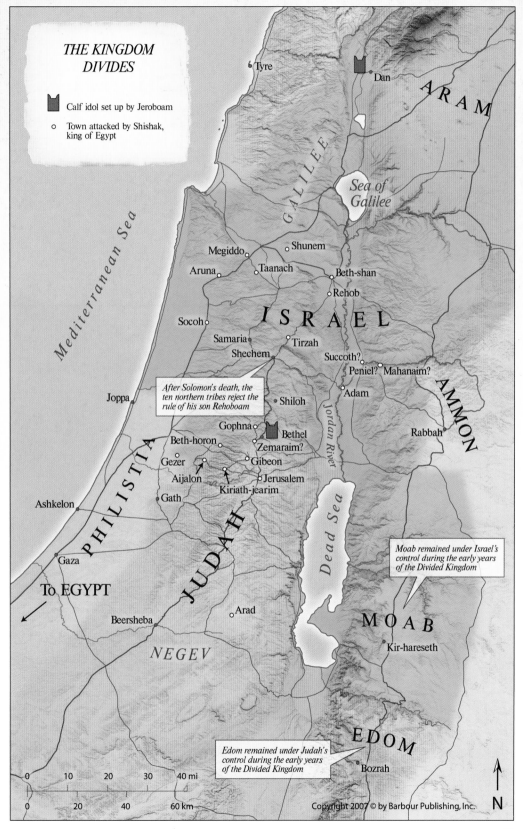

THE KINGDOM DIVIDES

■ Calf idol set up by Jeroboam

○ Town attacked by Shishak, king of Egypt

Tyre

Dan

ARAM

GALILEE

Sea of Galilee

Megiddo ○

Shunem

Aruna ○

Taanach ○

Beth-shan

Rehob

Socoh ○

I S R A E L

Samaria ○

Tirzah

Shechem

Succoth?

Peniel? Mahanaim?

After Solomon's death, the ten northern tribes reject the rule of his son Rehoboam

Joppa ○

Shiloh

Adam

Jordan River

AMMON

Gophna ○

Bethel ■

Beth-horon ○

Zemaraim?

Rabbah

Gezer ○

Gibeon ○

Aijalon ○

Jerusalem ○

Kiriath-jearim

Gath ○

Moab remained under Israel's control during the early years of the Divided Kingdom

Ashkelon ○

Mediterranean Sea

PHILISTIA

JUDAH

Dead Sea

Gaza ○

To EGYPT

Arad ○

M O A B

Beersheba ○

Kir-hareseth

N E G E V

EDOM

Edom remained under Judah's control during the early years of the Divided Kingdom

Bozrah

| 0 | 10 | 20 | 30 | 40 mi |

| 0 | 20 | 40 | 60 km |

N

ISRAEL'S WARS WITH ARAM

At war with King Baasha of the Northern Kingdom of Israel, King Asa of the Southern Kingdom of Judah refused to trust God for protection and instead made a treaty with Ben-Hadad (king of Damascus in Aram). The treaty effectively sandwiched the Northern Kingdom between two adversarial nations, causing the Northern Kingdom to end its siege on Judah.

During this period, Ben-hadad attacked and captured several cities in the Northern Kingdom, including the city of Dan (1 Kings 15:9–22).

Archaeologists have since reconstructed a portion of Dan's formidable fortifications (see photo).

Ben-hadad's son, Ben-hadad II, assembled a large army and led a series of attacks against the people of Israel (see lines on map). The blue line records a battle at Aphek where God fought for the Northern Kingdom (1 Kings 20). The red line recounts the battle for Samaria (2 Kings 6:24–33). The green line represents a battle between Aram and God's people (1 Kings 22); in this battle, Israel and Judah joined forces to repel the attacking Arameans, and King Ahab of Israel was killed by a "random" arrow shot into the battle.

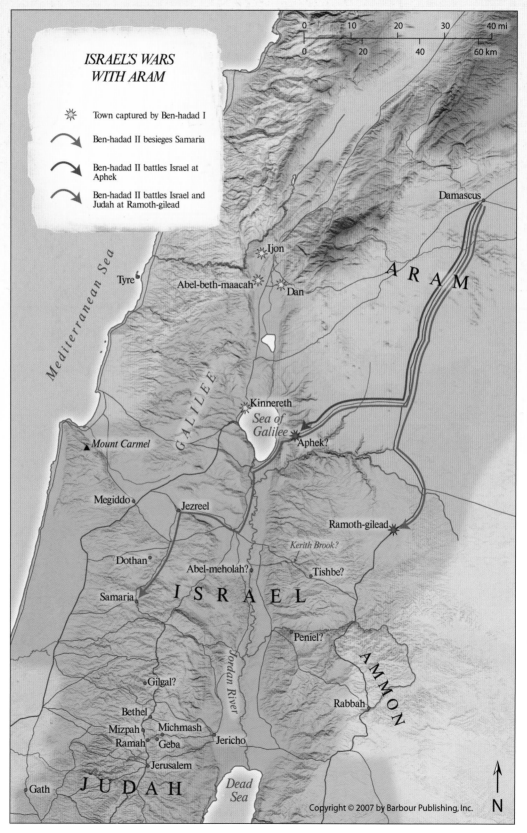

ISRAEL'S WARS
WITH ARAM

Town captured by Ben-hadad I

Ben-hadad II besieges Samaria

Ben-hadad II battles Israel at
Aphek

Ben-hadad II battles Israel and
Judah at Ramoth-gilead

Mediterranean Sea

Tyre

ARAM

Damascus

Ijon

Abel-beth-maacah

Dan

GALILEE

Kinnereth

Sea of
Galilee

Aphek?

Mount Carmel

Megiddo

Jezreel

Ramoth-gilead

Kerith Brook?

Dothan

Abel-meholah?

Tishbe?

Samaria

I S R A E L

Peniel?

AMMON

Jordan River

Gilgal?

Rabbah

Bethel

Mizpah   Michmash

Ramah   Geba

Jericho

Jerusalem

Gath   J U D A H

Dead
Sea

N

MOAB, EDOM, AND LIBNAH REVOLT

Within one hundred years of King Solomon's death, the reach and power of the Israelites began to wane. In a previous generation, a united kingdom had expanded its borders and ruled over neighboring nations. Now, with the kingdom divided and weakened, neighboring countries that had once paid tributes broke free and became hostile neighbors.

During the reign of Joram (also called Jehoram) of Israel, Moab stopped paying its yearly tribute of two hundred thousand animals. When they rebelled, King Joram allied with King Jehosaphat of Judah and together they attacked Kir-hareseth, the capital of Moab. While the city was well-situated and the rugged terrain gave it a good defense, the allied kings inflicted great casualties on the people of Moab (2 Kings 3). In the end, however, Moab still maintained its independence.

After Jehoshaphat's death, Jehoram became king of Judah. During his reign, Edom and their capital city of Bozrah (see photo) rebelled against the house of David, which still ruled Judah. In response, Jehoram mustered his army and traveled to the region of Edom. The Edomites won an initial strategic position and King Jehoram's army abandoned the cause and fled home. Thus, Edom secured its independence. Around the same time, the Levitical city of Libnah rebelled against Jehoram because of his disobedience to God's commands (2 Kings 8:22; 2 Chronicles 21:10).

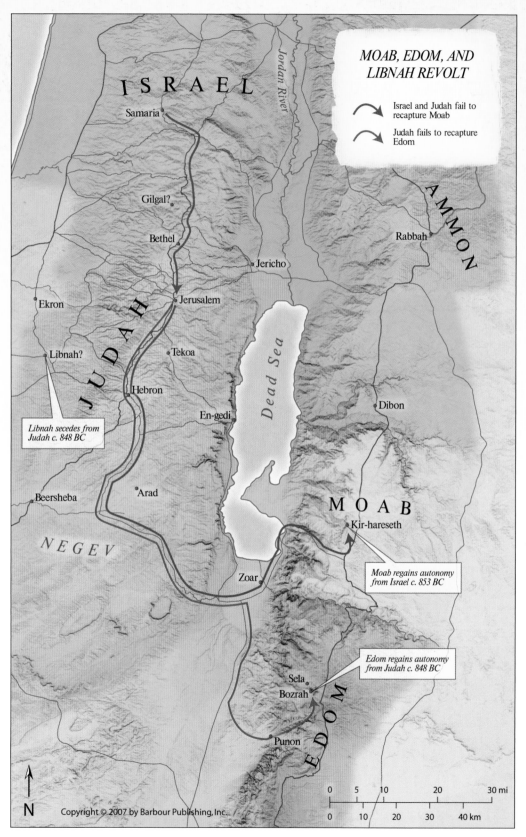

MOAB, EDOM, AND
LIBNAH REVOLT

Israel and Judah fail to
recapture Moab

Judah fails to recapture
Edom

ISRAEL

Samaria

Jordan River

Gilgal?

Bethel

Jericho

Rabbah

AMMON

Jerusalem

Ekron

JUDAH

Libnah?

Tekoa

Dead Sea

Dibon

Hebron

En-gedi

Libnah secedes from
Judah c. 848 BC

Beersheba

Arad

MOAB

Kir-hareseth

NEGEV

Moab regains autonomy
from Israel c. 853 BC

Zoar

Edom regains autonomy
from Judah c. 848 BC

Sela

Bozrah

EDOM

Punon

N

| 0 | 5 | 10 | 20 | 30 mi |

| 0 | 10 | 20 | 30 | 40 km |

EVENTS DURING JEHU'S REIGN

Injured in battle against the Arameans, King Joram of Israel traveled to Jezreel to recover from his wounds. While Joram recuperated, the prophet Elisha anointed Jehu as the new king of Israel. Jehu rallied his men, left the battle in Ramoth Gilead, and conspired to take the kingdom from Joram.

Jehu secured his reign by killing Joram, mortally wounding King Ahaziah of Judah, killing Jezebel, and slaughtering the many members of Ahab's and Ahaziah's families. Without any remaining competitors, Jehu assumed the throne in Samaria.

While Jehu succeeded in securing his place as king, he was less effective in securing the borders of Israel; he lost all the land east of the Jordan to Hazael, king of Aram. This fertile land, settled at one time by the tribe of Manasseh because of its ability to house large flocks, became the property of Aram (see photo). Read the story of Jehu in 2 Kings 9–10.

In addition to the biblical account, archaeological evidence indicates that the king of Assyria exacted a heavy and humiliating tribute from Jehu.

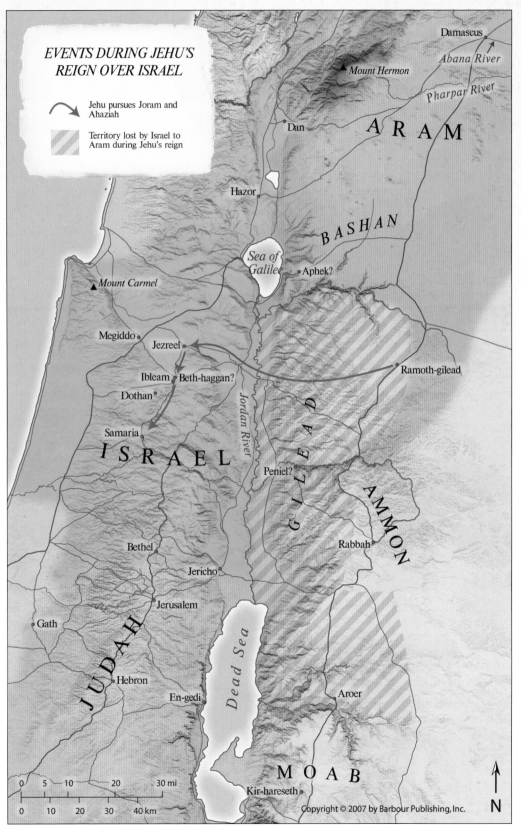

EVENTS DURING JEHU'S REIGN OVER ISRAEL

Jehu pursues Joram and Ahaziah

Territory lost by Israel to Aram during Jehu's reign

Damascus

Abana River

Pharpar River

Mount Hermon

Dan

A R A M

Hazor

BASHAN

Sea of Galilee

Aphek?

Mount Carmel

Megiddo

Jezreel

Ramoth-gilead

Ibleam · Beth-haggan?

Dothan

G I L E A D

Samaria

I S R A E L

Jordan River

Peniel?

A M M O N

Bethel

Rabbah

Jericho

Jerusalem

Gath

J U D A H

Dead Sea

Hebron

En-gedi

Aroer

M O A B

Kir-hareseth

0 5 10 20 30 mi
0 10 20 30 40 km

N

RESURGENCE DURING THE REIGNS OF JEROBOAM II AND AZARIAH

Jeroboam II reigned forty-one years as king of the Northern Kingdom. Best known for his military accomplishments, he "restored the boundaries of Israel from Lebo Hamath to the Sea of the Arabah [the Dead Sea]. . .he recovered for Israel both Damascus and Hamath" (2 Kings 14:25, 28). Jeroboam reigned during

a period of economic prosperity and was a contemporary of the prophets Hosea, Amos, and Jonah.

During the same time, Azariah (also called Uzziah) became king of the Southern Kingdom and reigned fifty-two years (see 2 Kings 15; 2 Chronicles 26). He also led his kingdom through a period of military and economic prosperity. He recaptured and rebuilt Elath, an important trading city on the Red Sea. He defeated the Philistine cities in the west (see photo for a view of this coastal region near Ashdod and Jabneh), the Arabs near Gurbaal, and the Meunites. "The Ammonites brought tribute to Uzziah, and his fame spread as far as the border of Egypt, because he had become very powerful" (2 Chronicles 26:8).

Unfortunately, his many successes gave him too much confidence, as 2 Chronicles 26:16 records: "But after Uzziah became powerful, his pride led to his downfall. He was unfaithful to the LORD his God, and entered the temple of the LORD to burn incense on the altar of incense." As a result of this sinful action, God struck Uzziah with leprosy and the king remained an outcast until he died.

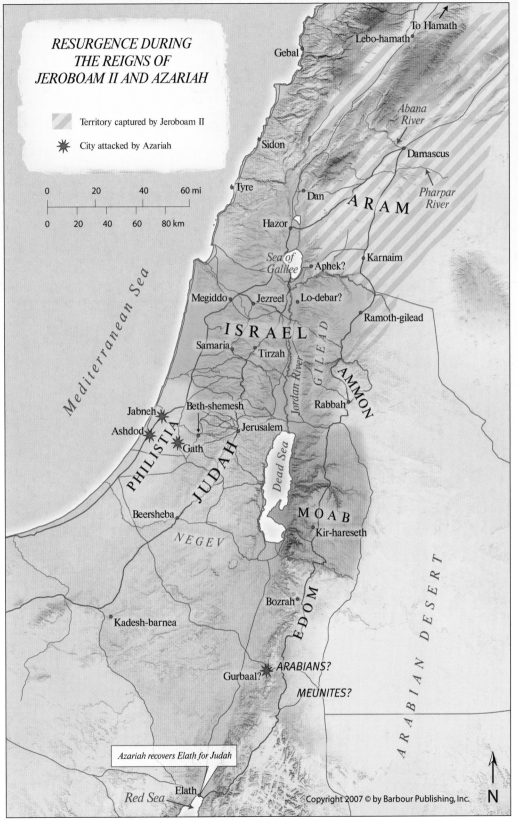

RESURGENCE DURING
THE REIGNS OF
JEROBOAM II AND AZARIAH

Territory captured by Jeroboam II

City attacked by Azariah

0   20   40   60 mi

0 20 40 60 80 km

To Hamath
Lebo-hamath
Gebal
Abana River
Sidon
Damascus
Tyre
Dan
ARAM
Pharpar River
Hazor
Sea of Galilee
Aphek?
Karnaim
Megiddo
Jezreel
Lo-debar?
Ramoth-gilead
ISRAEL
Samaria
Tirzah
GILEAD
AMMON
Jordan River
Beth-shemesh
Rabbah
Jabneh
Ashdod
Jerusalem
PHILISTIA
Gath
JUDAH
Dead Sea
Beersheba
MOAB
Kir-hareseth
NEGEV
EDOM
Bozrah
Kadesh-barnea
ARABIAN DESERT
ARABIANS?
Gurbaal?
MEUNITES?

Mediterranean Sea

Azariah recovers Elath for Judah

Red Sea
Elath

N

Copyright 2007 © by Barbour Publishing, Inc.

THE ASSYRIAN EMPIRE DURING 2 KINGS

Hoshea became the last king of Israel and reigned nine years before the Assyrian army conquered the Northern Kingdom. Assyria then deported the people of Israel and resettled the land with foreigners. The Bible clearly indicates that "all this took place because the Israelites had sinned against the LORD their God, who had brought them up out of Egypt" (2 Kings 17:7).

Here is a list of the kings of the Northern Kingdom before the Assyrian conquest:

Jeroboam I	1 Kings 11:26–40; 12–14; 2 Chronicles 10
Nadab	1 Kings 15:25–32
Baasha	1 Kings 15:33–16:7
Elah	1 Kings 16:8–14
Zimri	1 Kings 16:15–20
Tibni	1 Kings 16:21–22
Omri	1 Kings 16:15–28
Ahab	1 Kings 16–22; 2 Chronicles 18
Ahaziah	1 Kings 22:51–53; 2 Kings 1
Jehoram (Joram)	2 Kings 3, 9
Jehu	2 Kings 9–10
Jehoahaz	2 Kings 13:1–9
Jehoash	2 Kings 13:10–25
Jeroboam II	2 Kings 14:23–29
Zechariah	2 Kings 15:8–12
Shallum	2 Kings 15:10–16
Menahem	2 Kings 15:14–22
Pekahiah	2 Kings 15:22–26
Pekah	2 Kings 15:25–31
Hoshea	2 Kings 15:30; 17:1–6

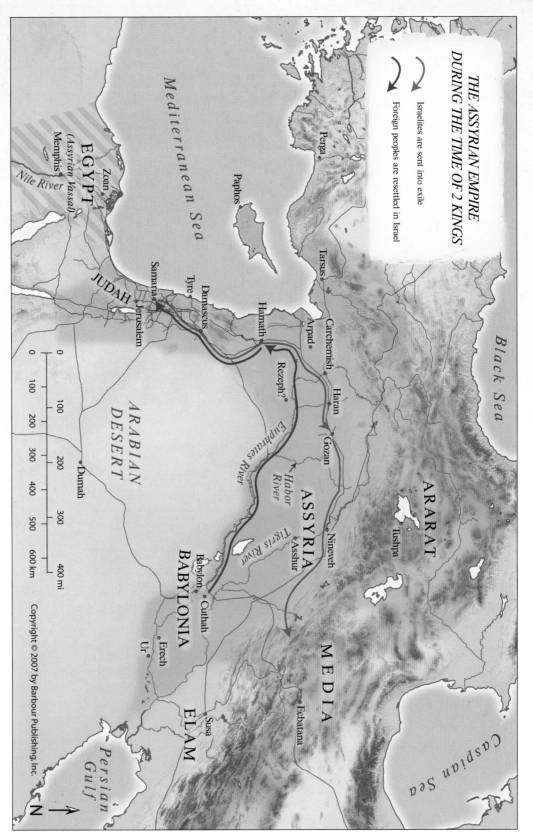

THE ASSYRIAN EMPIRE
DURING THE TIME OF 2 KINGS

Israelites are sent into exile

Foreign peoples are resettled in Israel

Mediterranean Sea

Perga

Paphos

Tarsus

Carchemish

Arpad

Haran

Samaria

Tyre

Damascus

JUDAH

Jerusalem

Hamath

Rezeph?

Gozan

Euphrates River

Habor River

ASSYRIA

Nineveh

Asshur

Tigris River

Babylon

Cuthah

BABYLONIA

Ur

Erech

Dumah

ARABIAN
DESERT

EGYPT

(Assyrian Vassal)

Memphis

Zoan

Nile River

ARARAT

Tushpa

Black Sea

MEDIA

Ecbatana

Susa

ELAM

Persian Gulf

Caspian Sea

0   100   200   300   400   500   600 km

0   100   200   300   400 mi

Copyright © 2007 by Barbour Publishing, Inc.

N

JERUSALEM DURING HEZEKIAH'S TIME

With the Northern Kingdom defeated and the people dispersed, the king of Assyria began also to threaten Judah with the same fate. In a dramatic confrontation that took place near the Upper Pool (see map), the people of Judah listened from the city wall and heard the taunts and threats of the Assyrian field commander, which he delivered to the king's officials in Hebrew.

Hezekiah responded to the Assyrian's challenge by praying to God. God answered his prayers with an encouraging prophecy from Isaiah. Soon afterward, an angel of the Lord struck the Assyrian camp, killing 185,000 soldiers, and King Sennacherib withdrew. (Read this story in 2 Kings 18–19. This event is also attested to by the ancient historian Herodotus.)

While the stories of his conquests, faith, and prayers have encouraged people throughout the centuries, Hezekiah also left behind one other lasting legacy. Second Kings 20:20 briefly mentions a water system created by Hezekiah. In 1838, western explorers discovered the 1,750 foot tunnel, which is considered one of the greatest feats of water engineering in the ancient world (see photo).

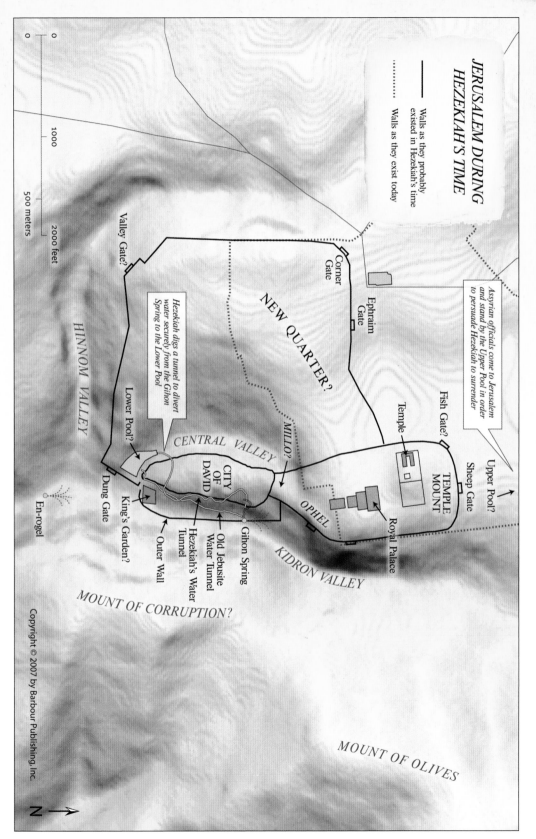

JERUSALEM DURING
HEZEKIAH'S TIME

Walls as they probably
existed in Hezekiah's time

Walls as they exist today

0   1000

0   500 meters

0   2000 feet

Assyrian officials come to Jerusalem
and stand by the Upper Pool in order
to persuade Hezekiah to surrender

Valley Gate?

Corner
Gate

Ephraim
Gate

NEW QUARTER?

Fish Gate?

Upper Pool?

Sheep Gate

Temple

TEMPLE
MOUNT

HINNOM VALLEY

Hezekiah digs a tunnel to divert
water securely from the Gihon
Spring to the Lower Pool

Lower Pool?

CENTRAL VALLEY

MILLO?

CITY
OF
DAVID

OPHEL

Royal Palace

En-rogel

Dung Gate

King's Garden?

Outer Wall

Hezekiah's Water
Tunnel

Old Jebusite
Water Tunnel

Gihon Spring

KIDRON VALLEY

MOUNT OF CORRUPTION?

Copyright © 2007 by Barbour Publishing, Inc.

N →

MOUNT OF OLIVES

91

EVENTS DURING JOSIAH'S REIGN OVER JUDAH

Although Assyria was the greatest military power in the region, it received growing pressure from Babylon. When the two powers began to engage in hostilities, the Assyrians called upon the king of Egypt, their vassal, to help defeat their enemies.

King Neco of Egypt quickly moved his armies along the most direct route to the battle, which took him through Josiah's Judah. Josiah mobilized for battle and opposed the Egyptians at Megiddo, where he was defeated and killed. King Neco continued to Carchemish but was himself met with defeat by Nebuchadnezzar's Babylonian army—the new, undisputed military power in the region. This photo shows arrowheads from the great battle at Carchemish, on display at the British Museum.

Despite his ill-fated decision to battle the Egyptians, Josiah was regarded as a good and effective king. He expanded the borders of the country, rid the land of idolatry, and worked at renewing the monotheistic religious practices of the people of Judah. Read his story in 2 Kings 22:1–23:30 and 2 Chronicles 34–35.

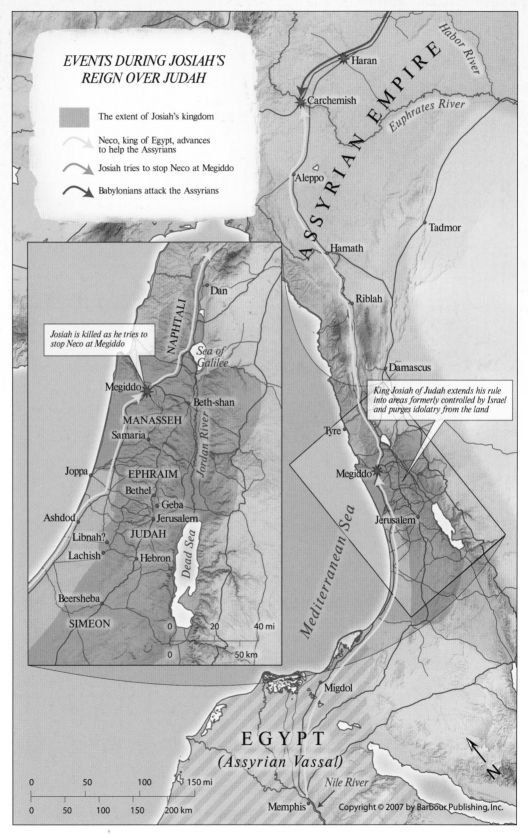

EVENTS DURING JOSIAH'S REIGN OVER JUDAH

The extent of Josiah's kingdom

Neco, king of Egypt, advances to help the Assyrians

Josiah tries to stop Neco at Megiddo

Babylonians attack the Assyrians

Habor River

Haran

Carchemish

ASSYRIAN EMPIRE

Euphrates River

Aleppo

Tadmor

Hamath

Riblah

Dan

NAPHTALI

Sea of Galilee

Josiah is killed as he tries to stop Neco at Megiddo

Damascus

Megiddo

Beth-shan

King Josiah of Judah extends his rule into areas formerly controlled by Israel and purges idolatry from the land

MANASSEH

Samaria

Tyre

Joppa

EPHRAIM

Megiddo

Bethel

Geba

Ashdod

Jerusalem

Jerusalem

Libnah?

JUDAH

Lachish

Hebron

Dead Sea

Mediterranean Sea

Jordan River

Beersheba

SIMEON

| 0 | 20 | 40 mi |
| 0 | | 50 km |

Migdol

EGYPT
(Assyrian Vassal)

N

| 0 | 50 | 100 | 150 mi |
| 0 | 50 | 100 | 150 | 200 km |

Nile River

Memphis

Copyright © 2007 by Barbour Publishing, Inc.

THE BABYLONIAN EMPIRE DURING 2 KINGS

Though the southern kingdom of Judah outlasted the Northern Kingdom, it eventually fell to the Babylonian Empire and its people were sent into exile. Unlike most of their brothers to the north, many citizens of the Southern Kingdom eventually returned to the promised land. Below is a list of kings (and one queen) who ruled the Southern Kingdom of Judah before the people were exiled.

Rehoboam	1 Kings 12:1–24; 14:21–31; 2 Chronicles 10–12
Abijah	1 Kings 15:1–8; 2 Chronicles 13
Asa	1 Kings 15:9–24; 2 Chronicles 14–16
Jehoshaphat	1 Kings 22; 2 Chronicles 17–20
Joram (Jehoram)	2 Kings 8:16–24; 2 Chronicles 21
Ahaziah	2 Kings 8:25–29; 2 Chronicles 22:1–9
Queen Athaliah	2 Kings 11; 2 Chronicles 22:10– 23:21
Joash	2 Kings 12; 2 Chronicles 24
Amaziah	2 Kings 14:1–22; 2 Chronicles 25
Azariah (Uzziah)	2 Kings 15:1–7; 2 Chronicles 26
Jotham	2 Kings 15:32–38; 2 Chronicles 27
Ahaz	2 Kings 16; 2 Chronicles 28
Hezekiah	2 Kings 18–20; 2 Chronicles 29–32; Isaiah 36–39
Manasseh	2 Kings 21:1–18; 2 Chronicles 33:1–20
Amon	2 Kings 21:19–26; 2 Chronicles 33:21–25
Josiah	2 Kings 22:1–23:30; 2 Chronicles 34–35
Jehoahaz	2 Kings 23:31–35; 2 Chronicles 36:1–4
Jehoiakim	2 Kings 23:36–24:6; 2 Chronicles 36:5–8
Jehoiachin	2 Kings 24:8–17, 25:27–30; 2 Chronicles 36:9–10
Zedekiah	2 Kings 24:18–25:7; 2 Chronicles 36:11–14

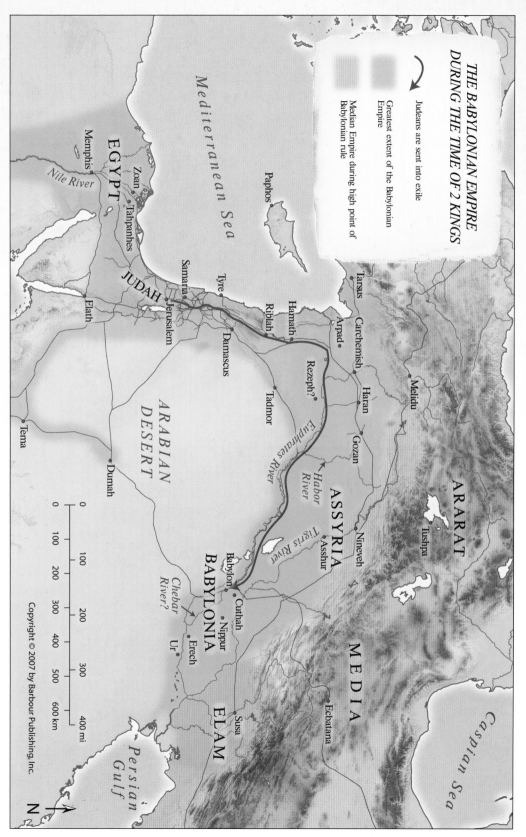

THE BABYLONIAN EMPIRE
DURING THE TIME OF 2 KINGS

Judeans are sent into exile

Greatest extent of the Babylonian
Empire

Median Empire during high point of
Babylonian rule

Mediterranean Sea

EGYPT

Memphis
Nile River
Zoan
Tahpanhes

Elath

JUDAH
Jerusalem
Samaria

Tyre

Paphos

Damascus

Hamath
Riblah

Tadmor

Rezeph?

ARABIAN
DESERT

Tema

Dumah

Tarsus
Carchemish
Arpad

Haran

Melidu

Gozan

Euphrates River

Habor
River

Tigris River

ASSYRIA

Nineveh
Asshur

Tushpa

ARARAT

Babylon

BABYLONIA

Chebar
River?

Nippur
Cuthah

Ur
Erech

ELAM

Susa

Ecbatana

M E D I A

Caspian Sea

Persian
Gulf

N

0 100 200 300 400 500 600 km
0 100 200 300 400 mi

ISRAEL DURING THE TIME OF 1 CHRONICLES

Below are key events in the history of the Hebrew monarchy:	
1051 BC	Saul becomes the first king of Israel.
1011 BC	David becomes king of Judah.
960 BC	The first temple is built in Jerusalem, replacing the tabernacle built by Moses (see photos of reconstruction of Tabernacle).
930 BC	The kingdom divides into two countries. The northern is known as Israel, and the southern is known as Judah.
722 BC	The ten tribes of the Northern Kingdom are conquered by Assyria and driven into exile. These tribes never return.
586 BC	The southern kingdom of Judah falls to Babylon.

The biblical timeline continues on page 106.

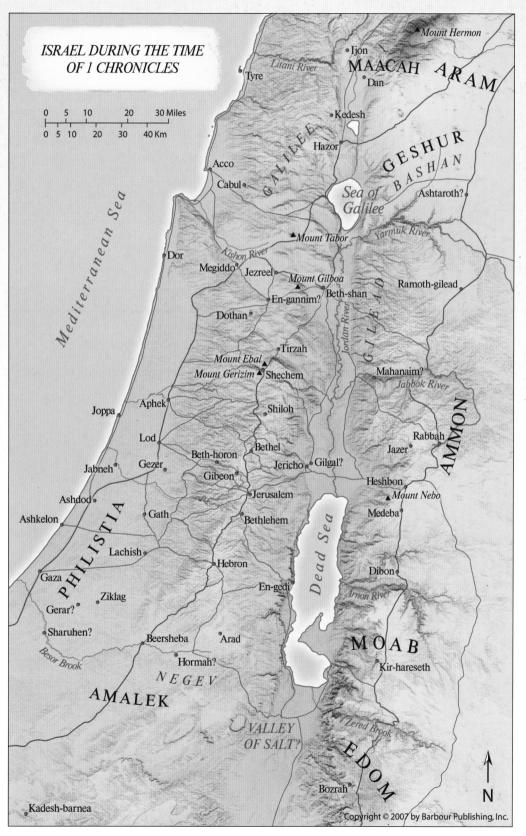

ISRAEL DURING THE TIME
OF 1 CHRONICLES

0   5   10   20   30 Miles
0 5 10   20   30   40 Km

Mediterranean Sea

Mount Hermon

Ijon

MAACAH   ARAM

Tyre

Litani River

Dan

Kedesh

GESHUR

Hazor

BASHAN

Acco

GALILEE

Cabul

Sea of
Galilee

Ashtaroth?

Mount Tabor

Yarmuk River

Dor

Kishon River

Megiddo

Jezreel

Mount Gilboa

Beth-shan

GILEAD

Ramoth-gilead

En-gannim?

Dothan

Jordan River

Tirzah

Mount Ebal

Shechem

Mahanaim?

Mount Gerizim

Jabbok River

Shiloh

AMMON

Joppa

Aphek

Lod

Bethel

Rabbah

Jazer

Beth-horon

Jericho   Gilgal?

Gezer

Gibeon

Heshbon

Jabneh

Jerusalem

Mount Nebo

Ashdod

Gath

Medeba

Ashkelon

Bethlehem

PHILISTIA

Dead Sea

Lachish

Hebron

Dibon

Gaza

En-gedi

Ziklag

Arnon River

Gerar?

Sharuhen?

Beersheba

Arad

MOAB

Bezor Brook

Hormah?

Kir-hareseth

NEGEV

AMALEK

Zered Brook

VALLEY
OF SALT?

EDOM

Bozrah

N

Kadesh-barnea

EVENTS DURING ASA'S REIGN

During the rule of Asa, the Ethiopians attacked Judah. Coming from the south, Zerah led a sizeable army of the Ethiopians (also called the Cushites) into the southern portion of Judah.

In response, Asa mustered his own army, numbering 300,000 men, to battle the Ethiopians near Mareshah. Asa's army defeated his enemies, drove them back to Gerar, and eventually annihilated them. During the battle, Asa's armies also conquered the cities near Gerar, carrying off a substantial amount of plunder.

Despite the fact that this region was in the dry Negev, it received enough rainfall to produce a plentiful harvest of fruits, grains, and vegetables (see photo of Gerar)—creating great wealth that became the property of Asa and his men. "They destroyed all the villages around Gerar, for the terror of the LORD had fallen upon them. They plundered all these villages, since there was much booty there. They also attacked the camps of the herdsmen and carried off droves of sheep and goats and camels. Then they returned to Jerusalem" (2 Chronicles 14:14–15).

Read the entire story in 2 Chronicles 14.

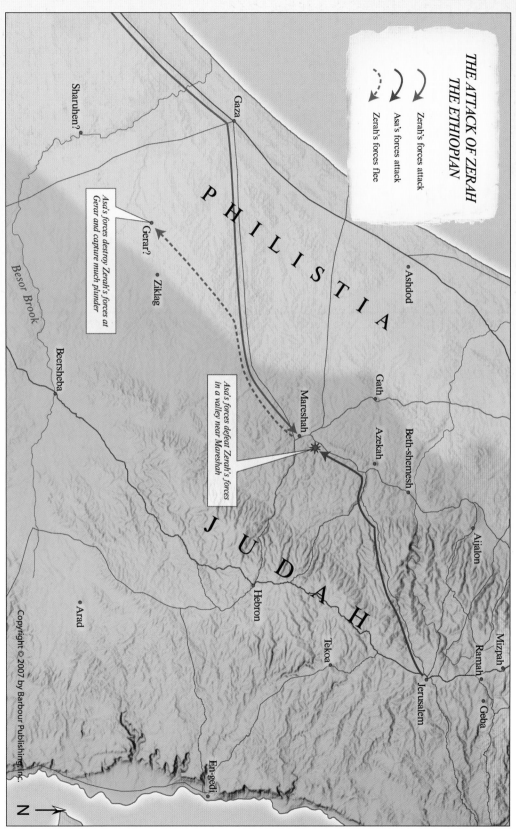

THE ATTACK OF ZERAH
THE ETHIOPIAN

Zerah's forces attack

Asa's forces attack

Zerah's forces flee

Asa's forces destroy Zerah's forces at Gerar and capture much plunder

Asa's forces defeat Zerah's forces in a valley near Mareshah

Gaza

Sharuhen?

Besor Brook

Gerar?

Ziklag

Beersheba

Arad

P H I L I S T I A

Ashdod

Gath

Azekah

Beth-shemesh

Mareshah

J U D A H

Hebron

Tekoa

En-gedi

Aijalon

Mizpah
Ramah
Geba

Jerusalem

N →

EVENTS DURING JEHOSHAPHAT'S REIGN OVER JUDAH

Though it regards Jehoshaphat as a good king, the biblical account of his reign reveals a man with a flawed record of devotion to God.

On the positive side, the biblical writers commend Jehoshaphat for his faith in God during a battle with the Moabites. When his enemies assembled a coalition of countries to fight against him, Jehoshaphat rallied the people to pray for God's help. God intervened by defeating the enemy while the army of Judah simply stood by and watched. While Jehoshaphat's soldiers awaited the battle, the enemy coalition fell apart as the allied countries began attacking each other rather than the Judeans (2 Chronicles 20:23).

On the negative side, the biblical accounts condemn Jehoshaphat for the alliance he made with King Ahaziah of the Northern Kingdom. Though this partnership must have seemed expedient, God did not approve of the alliance. God disciplined Jehoshaphat by destroying his merchant ships and long-term trading plans for Ezion-geber. A large storm likely blew up on the Red Sea (see photo) and destroyed the ships being built. While it might be easy to ascribe the cause of this event to merely natural phenomena, we learn in 1 Kings 22:48 and 2 Chronicles 20:37 that this was clearly an act of divine judgment.

Shortly after Jehoshaphat's death, his son Jehoram became king. Around this time, Moab rebelled from Israel, and Edom and Libnah revolted from Judah.

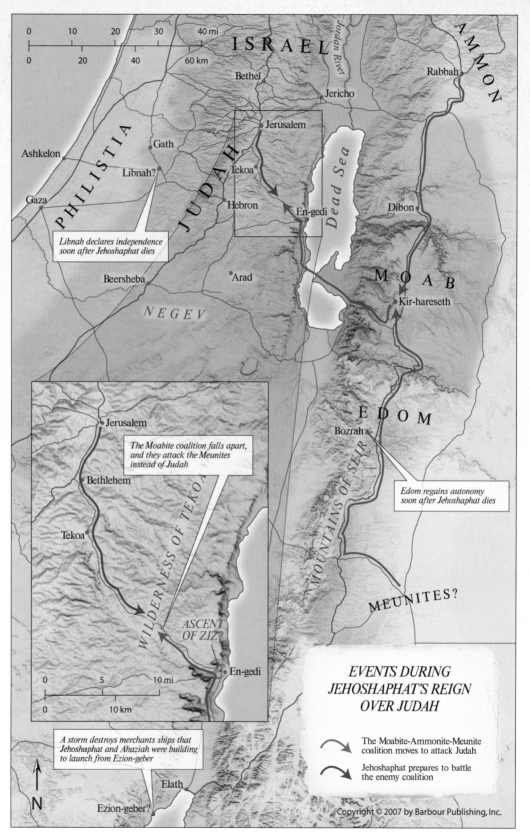

ISRAEL

Bethel

Jericho

Jordan River

AMMON

Rabbah

Jerusalem

Dead Sea

Ashkelon

Gath

PHILISTIA

Libnah?

JUDAH

Tekoa

Gaza

Hebron

En-gedi

Dibon

Libnah declares independence
soon after Jehoshaphat dies

Beersheba

*Arad

NEGEV

MOAB

Kir-hareseth

EDOM

Bozrah

Jerusalem

The Moabite coalition falls apart,
and they attack the Meunites
instead of Judah

Bethlehem

MOUNTAINS OF SEIR

Edom regains autonomy
soon after Jehoshaphat dies

Tekoa

WILDERNESS OF TEKOA

MEUNITES?

*ASCENT
OF ZIZ?*

En-gedi

0   5   10 mi

0   10 km

A storm destroys merchants ships that
Jehoshaphat and Ahaziah were building
to launch from Ezion-geber

N

Elath

Ezion-geber?

*EVENTS DURING
JEHOSHAPHAT'S REIGN
OVER JUDAH*

The Moabite-Ammonite-Meunite
coalition moves to attack Judah

Jehoshaphat prepares to battle
the enemy coalition

Copyright © 2007 by Barbour Publishing, Inc.

101

ARAM AND ISRAEL ATTACK JUDAH

Though not particularly well-known, Ahaz was certainly one of the most influential kings in Judah's history.

Spiritually, the biblical writers described Ahaz as an evil king who went as far as sacrificing his own son to pagan gods. As Ahaz faced attacks from all sides, the Bible says, "The LORD had humbled Judah because of Ahaz king of Israel, for he had promoted wickedness in Judah and had been most unfaithful to the Lord" (2 Chronicles 28:19). Toward the end of his reign, he closed the temple and set up altars to other gods throughout the land.

Militarily, the country of Judah was squeezed. While the Philistines captured cities in western Judah, Israel put pressure on them from the north. At the same time, Aram also attacked. Judah faced high casualty losses; in one battle with Israel the Judeans lost 120,000 men in the span of just one day.

Desperate, Ahaz sent for help from Assyria. The Assyrians arrived and defeated the invading armies, but they exacted a high cost for their help. Four long-term consequences resulted from Ahaz's actions:

1) Assyria stripped Judah of many financial resources.
2) The treasured city of Elath, known for its important trading port (see photo), was lost.
3) Assyria grew more powerful in the region.
4) By coming to the rescue of Judah, Assyria decimated the northern kingdom of Israel—eventually ending its very existence a few years later.

Read the full story in 2 Kings 16, 2 Chronicles 28, and Isaiah 7.

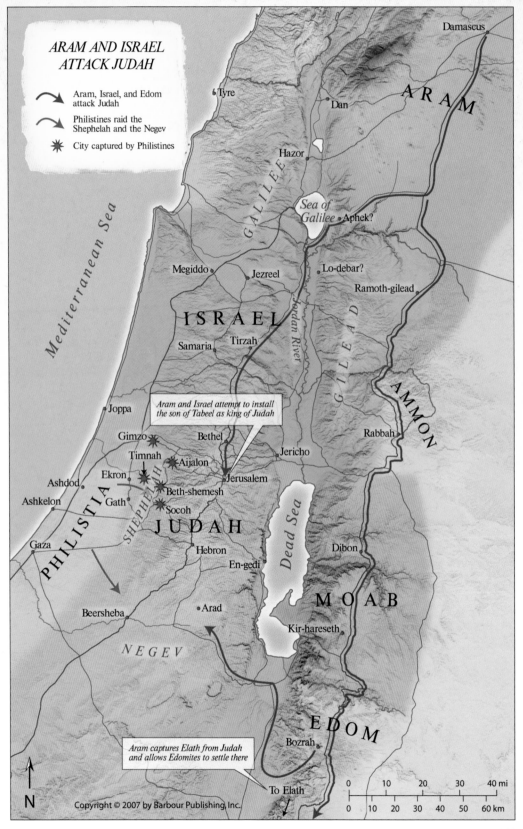

ARAM AND ISRAEL
ATTACK JUDAH

Aram, Israel, and Edom
attack Judah

Philistines raid the
Shephelah and the Negev

City captured by Philistines

Damascus

Tyre

Dan

A R A M

Hazor

GALILEE

Sea of
Galilee • Aphek?

Mediterranean Sea

Megiddo

Jezreel

Lo-debar?

Ramoth-gilead

I S R A E L

Jordan River

G I L E A D

A M M O N

Samaria

Tirzah

Rabbah

Joppa

Aram and Israel attempt to install
the son of Tabeel as king of Judah

Gimzo

Bethel

Jericho

Timnah

Aijalon

Ekron

Jerusalem

Ashdod

SHEPHELAH

Beth-shemesh

Ashkelon

Gath

Socoh

Dibon

J U D A H

Dead Sea

Gaza

PHILISTIA

Hebron

En-gedi

M O A B

Beersheba

Arad

Kir-hareseth

N E G E V

E D O M

Bozrah

Aram captures Elath from Judah
and allows Edomites to settle there

N

Copyright © 2007 by Barbour Publishing, Inc.

To Elath

0   10   20   30   40 mi

0   10   20   30   40   50   60 km

EZRA LEADS EXILES BACK TO JUDEA

Although the Southern Kingdom had fallen and the people were taken away into captivity, God eventually brought them back to Judah (now called Judea), and the king of Persia commissioned a group of Jewish people to begin temple reconstruction. This account was consistent with the Persian practice of encouraging local worship within the regions they ruled. The Persian kings had preserved the treasures of the Hebrew temple and were ready to restore those treasures to the rebuilt temple.

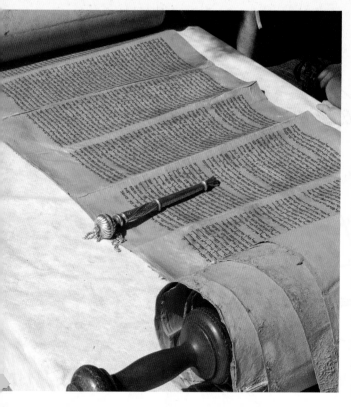

Zerubbabel led the initial group of exiles back to Jerusalem. They began construction on the temple—laying the foundation in an emotional ceremony (Ezra 3:13). Work continued intermittently because of local pressures and opposition.

When the temple was finally completed, Ezra, a priest, led another group of Jewish people back to Jerusalem. With letters of endorsement and treasures from the king, Ezra returned to Jerusalem. With a deep understanding of and respect for the Law of Moses, Ezra helped the people restore proper Jewish practices.

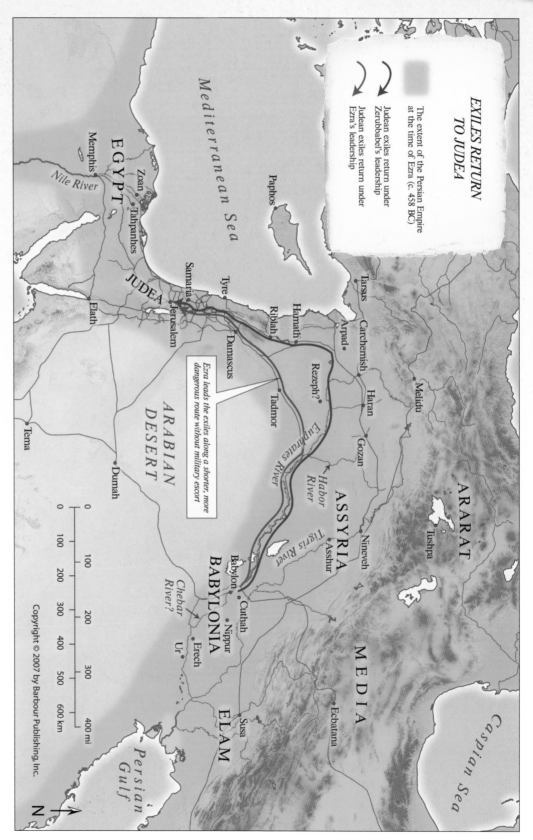

EXILES RETURN TO JUDEA

The extent of the Persian Empire at the time of Ezra (c. 458 BC)

Judean exiles return under Zerubbabel's leadership

Judean exiles return under Ezra's leadership

Ezra leads the exiles along a shorter, more dangerous route without military escort

Mediterranean Sea

EGYPT

Memphis

Nile River

Zoan

Tahpanhes

Paphos

Elath

JUDEA

Jerusalem

Samaria

Tyre

Damascus

Riblah

Hamath

Arpad

Tarsus

Carchemish

Haran

Melidu

Rezeph?

Tadmor

Gozan

ARABIAN DESERT

Euphrates River

Habor River

ASSYRIA

Nineveh

Asshur

Tigris River

Tushpa

ARARAT

Tema

Dumah

Chebar River?

BABYLONIA

Babylon

Cuthah

Nippur

Ur

Erech

ELAM

Susa

Ecbatana

MEDIA

Persian Gulf

Caspian Sea

0   100 200 300 400 500 600 km
0   100   200   300   400 mi

N

JUDEA DURING NEHEMIAH'S TIME

A cover-to-cover reading of the Bible doesn't yield all the information needed to understand the historical context of every book. The chart below chronologically portrays the order of events surrounding the Jewish exile. While many scholars disagree about the exact date and year of each event, the general flow of events is not usually challenged.

Key events between the exile of the Southern Kingdom and the work of Nehemiah
586 BC Nebuchadnezzar destroys Jerusalem and the temple. The Jewish people are deported to Babylon. Daniel serves as advisor to the kings of Babylon (and later of the Medes and Persians).
554 BC Belshazzar begins to reign in Babylon.
539 BC Cyrus the Mede conquers Babylon and sets up Darius as regional king. Daniel and the Jewish exiles are now subjects in the empire of the Medes and Persians.
538 BC Zerubbabel brings a contingent of exiled Jewish people back to Israel. Temple reconstruction begins soon after.
520 BC Zechariah and Haggai prophesy.
516 BC The temple reconstruction is completed.
486 BC Xerxes becomes king of Persia.
478 BC Esther becomes queen of Persia.
464 BC Artaxerxes assumes the throne in Persia.
458 BC Ezra leads additional exiled Jews back to Judea.
445 BC Nehemiah is commissioned to rebuild the walls.
425 BC Malachi prophesies.

The biblical timeline continues on page 146.

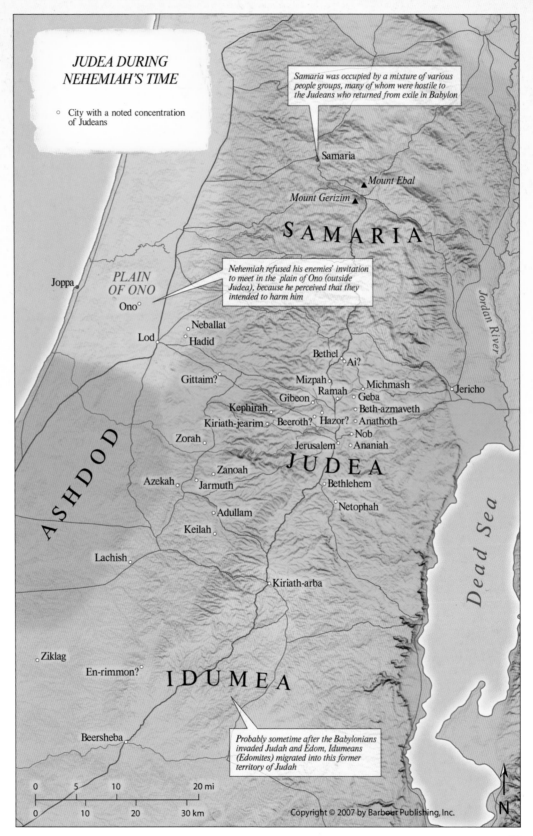

JUDEA DURING NEHEMIAH'S TIME

○ City with a noted concentration of Judeans

Samaria was occupied by a mixture of various people groups, many of whom were hostile to the Judeans who returned from exile in Babylon

Samaria

▲ *Mount Ebal*

Mount Gerizim ▲

SAMARIA

Jordan River

Joppa

PLAIN OF ONO

Ono ○

Nehemiah refused his enemies' invitation to meet in the plain of Ono (outside Judea), because he perceived that they intended to harm him

Neballat ○

Lod

○ Hadid

Bethel

○ Ai?

Gittaim? ○

Mizpah ○

○ Michmash

Ramah ○

Gibeon ○

○ Geba

Kephirah ○

○ Beth-azmaveth

Kiriath-jearim ○

Beeroth? ○

Hazor? ○

Anathoth

○ Nob

Zorah ○

Jerusalem ○

○ Ananiah

JUDEA

Jericho ○

Zanoah ○

Azekah ○

Jarmuth ○

○ Bethlehem

ASHDOD

Adullam ○

○ Netophah

Keilah ○

Lachish ○

Dead Sea

○ Kiriath-arba

Ziklag ○

En-rimmon? ○

IDUMEA

Probably sometime after the Babylonians invaded Judah and Edom, Idumeans (Edomites) migrated into this former territory of Judah

Beersheba ○

0   5   10   20 mi

0   10   20   30 km

Copyright © 2007 by Barbour Publishing, Inc.

N

NEHEMIAH REBUILDS JERUSALEM'S WALLS

Though glad to have the temple completed, the people of Jerusalem found themselves in a vulnerable position with the city walls still in ruins. Nehemiah, a Jew serving in Artaxerxes' court, petitioned the king—who granted his request—to lead a contingent back to Jerusalem to rebuild the city walls. The king gave Nehemiah letters guaranteeing his protection and providing the necessary supplies.

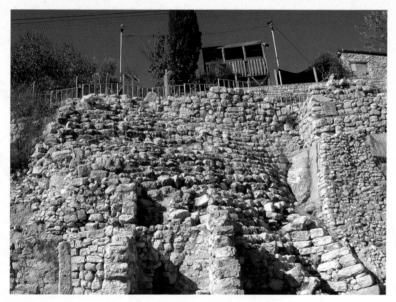

Nehemiah motivated the people to begin the effort of rebuilding the walls. When local troublemakers opposed them, the workers continued their task wearing swords in order to fend off their antagonists. Working nonstop, they completed the walls in a remarkably short time. The book of Nehemiah records that "the wall was completed. . .in fifty-two days. When all our enemies heard about this, all the surrounding nations were afraid and lost their self-confidence, because they realized that this work had been done with the help of our God" (Nehemiah 6:15–16).

With the wall completed, the people rededicated themselves to their faith in God as Ezra the priest read the Torah to the people. After the people had dedicated themselves, they also dedicated the walls of Jerusalem. This included having two choirs of Levites march along the city walls giving thanks to God (Nehemiah 12:27–47).

The tower on the right side of the photograph is believed to be remaining from the time of Nehemiah.

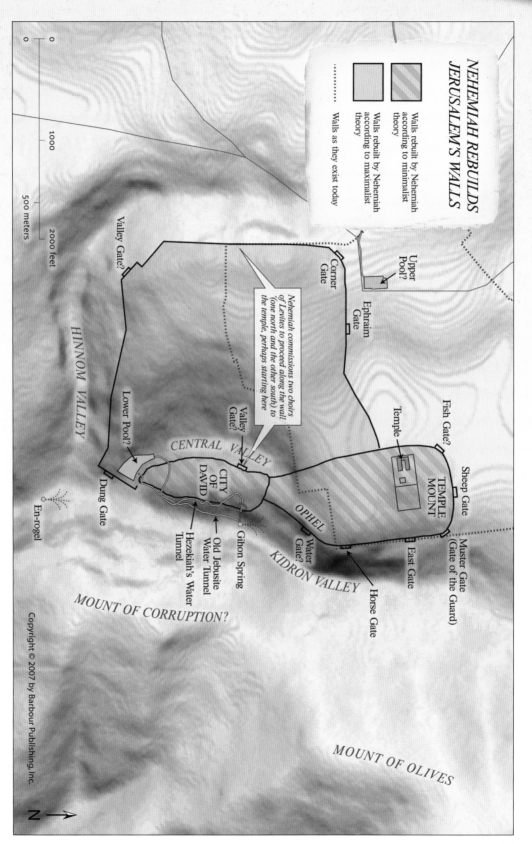

NEHEMIAH REBUILDS
JERUSALEM'S WALLS

Walls rebuilt by Nehemiah according to minimalist theory

Walls rebuilt by Nehemiah according to maximalist theory

Walls as they exist today

Nehemiah commissions two choirs of Levites to proceed along the wall (one north and the other south) to the temple, perhaps starting here

0
0

1000

500 meters

2000 feet

Valley Gate?

Corner Gate

Upper Pool?

Ephraim Gate

HINNOM VALLEY

Lower Pool?

Valley Gate?

CENTRAL VALLEY

Temple

Fish Gate?

TEMPLE MOUNT

Sheep Gate

Muster Gate
(Gate of the Guard)

Dung Gate

En-rogel

CITY OF DAVID

Hezekiah's Water Tunnel

Old Jebusite Water Tunnel

Gihon Spring

OPHEL

Water Gate?

East Gate

Horse Gate

KIDRON VALLEY

MOUNT OF CORRUPTION?

MOUNT OF OLIVES

N →

THE PERSIAN EMPIRE DURING ESTHER'S TIME

While the story of Esther is enjoyed as one of the great dramas of the Bible, few readers understand that the world was at a historical crossroads during this time.

The Persian Empire extended from India to Ethiopia—even Egypt had fallen to the Persians. When the Persian Empire was at its height, major cultural developments were taking place

throughout the world. Around the same time that Esther lived in Persia, Confucius lived in China, Buddha lived in India, and Socrates lived in Greece.

While Esther was alive, this gold relief panel (photo) was on display in Susa—the capital of the Persian Empire. Also during her lifetime, King Xerxes led the Persian army west in an effort to enter Europe and conquer Greece. The city states of Greece united to fight, hold off, and eventually defeat the Persians— handing them their first major military defeat. Had the Persians won that battle, their influence would have extended well into Europe. Instead, the Greek victory allowed the Greek culture and influence to rise and ultimately shape modern western civilization.

THE PERSIAN EMPIRE
DURING ESTHER'S TIME

Extent of the Persian
Empire at the time of
Esther (c. 480 BC)

Territories of the
Hellenic League

Esther reigned as queen in
the capital city of Susa

III

THE SETTING OF JOB

Job lived during a time when wealth was not measured in shekels or dollars but in herds and livestock. Job's thousands of sheep, oxen, and donkeys indicated that he was very, very rich.

Job's story is one of the most well-known in the Bible. His faith in God was tested when his children were killed and his wealth stripped from him. Job cursed the day he was born, yet he never disavowed his allegiance to God. In the end, God rewarded Job's faith by granting him a new family and doubling his original wealth.

Though the exact time of Job's story isn't known, the emphasis on livestock as a measurement of wealth seems to indicate that the story took place during or before the time of Abraham. And while the exact location of Job's story isn't indicated either, the presence of Sabean and Chaldean raiders suggest that Uz is located as indicated on the map.

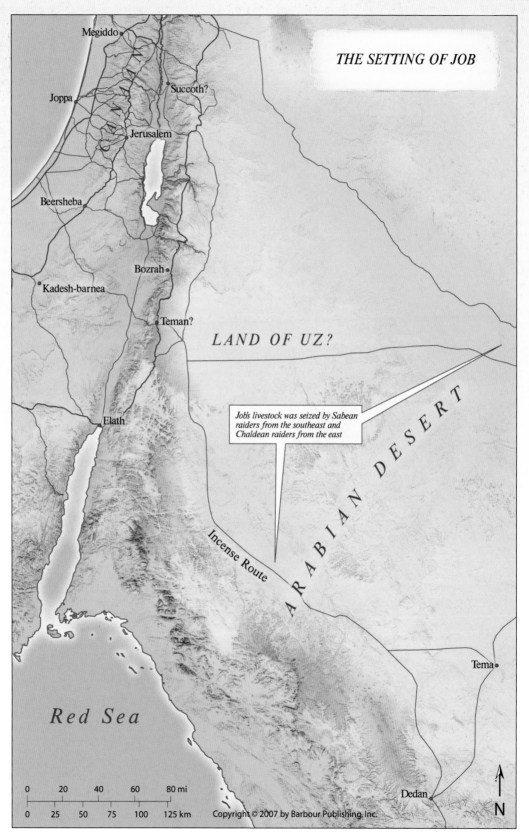

THE SETTING OF JOB

Megiddo

Joppa

Succoth?

Jerusalem

Beersheba

Bozrah

Kadesh-barnea

Teman?

LAND OF UZ?

Job's livestock was seized by Sabean raiders from the southeast and Chaldean raiders from the east

Elath

A R A B I A N   D E S E R T

Incense Route

Red Sea

Tema

0   20   40   60   80 mi

0   25   50   75   100   125 km

Copyright © 2007 by Barbour Publishing, Inc.

Dedan

N

THE PROPHETS

ASSYRIA ADVANCES ON JERUSALEM

Isaiah warned Israel of the impending danger from Assyria. The Judean oppression of the poor—depriving the needy of their rights—fueled God's discipline (Isaiah 10). Isaiah warned that nothing would save the Southern Kingdom from the coming judgment. When the people looked back and wondered why God allowed them to fall to the Assyrians, they would remember Isaiah's prophecy.

Were the Assyrians God's new people? No, they were merely the instrument God used to dole out His judgment (Isaiah 10:5). In fact, God pledged to discipline the Assyrians as well for their arrogance and pride. "When the Lord has finished all his work against Mount Zion and Jerusalem, he will say, 'I will punish the king of Assyria for the willfull pride of his heart and the haughty look in his eyes' " (Isaiah 10:12).

The map indicates the route the Assyrian army would take as envisioned by Isaiah. Michmash (see photo) stood at a natural crossroads that made it a strategic location on the north/south route through the land. For this reason, it was the location of several important battles (see page 54) and a tactical place for storing supplies (Isaiah 10:28).

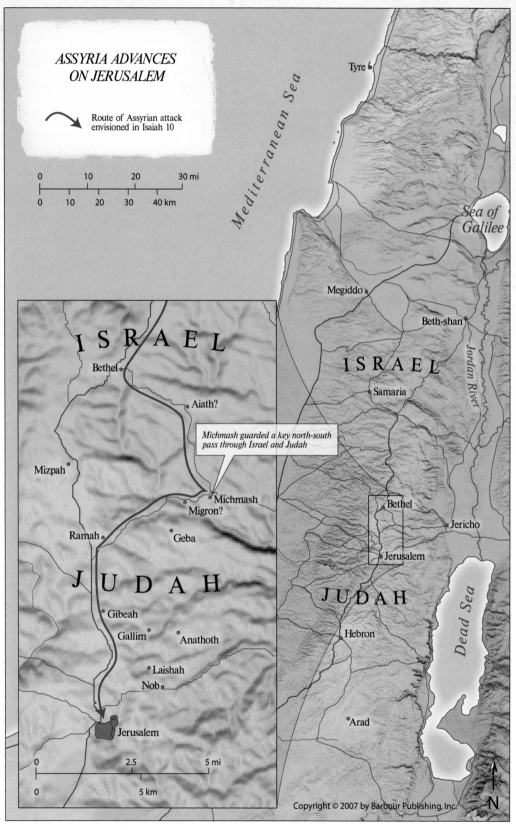

ASSYRIA ADVANCES
ON JERUSALEM

Route of Assyrian attack
envisioned in Isaiah 10

0   10   20   30 mi

0 10 20 30 40 km

Mediterranean Sea

Tyre

Sea of
Galilee

Megiddo

Beth-shan

ISRAEL

Samaria

Jordan River

ISRAEL

Bethel

Aiath?

Michmash guarded a key north-south
pass through Israel and Judah

Mizpah

Michmash

Migron?

Bethel

Jericho

Ramah

Geba

Jerusalem

JUDAH

JUDAH

Gibeah

Gallim

Anathoth

Hebron

Laishah

Nob

Dead Sea

Jerusalem

Arad

0   2.5   5 mi

0   5 km

N

PROPHECIES AGAINST MOAB

After the death of Ahab, Moab revolted against Israel's rule and gained independence. Even though Moab experienced immediate success in expanding its borders, Isaiah prophesied against the land of Moab and revealed that disaster would swiftly fall upon it (see Isaiah 15:1–16:4).

Moab contained diverse terrain—including both plush, green pastures and dry rocky areas (see photos). Moab is also distinguished in the Bible as the homeland of Ruth.

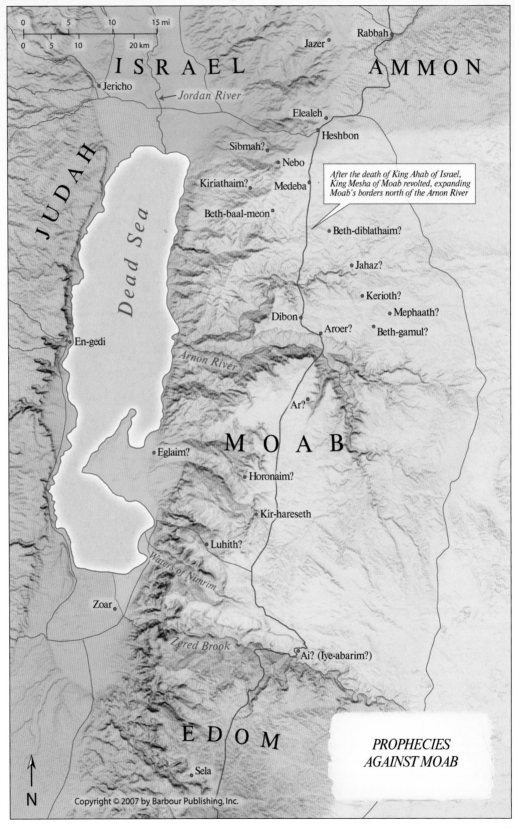

After the death of King Ahab of Israel, King Mesha of Moab revolted, expanding Moab's borders north of the Arnon River

PROPHECIES AGAINST MOAB

Copyright © 2007 by Barbour Publishing, Inc.

GEDALIAH'S ASSASSINATION

Jeremiah eventually witnessed the fall of Jerusalem to Nebuchadnezzar's mighty Babylonian Empire. This empire was the dominant power in the Near East during this time. Without the luxuries of modern-day travel or communication, however, Nebuchadnezzar faced the challenges of ruling a vast empire from his own capital city. Because he needed a ruler who would stay faithful to him, the Babylonian king appointed Gedaliah to rule Judah.

Gedaliah tried to create order by assuring the Judeans who remained in the land, "Do not be afraid to serve the Babylonians. . . . Settle down in the land and serve the king of Babylon, and it will go well with you" (Jeremiah 40:9).

But Ishmael, a member of the Ammonite royal family, assassinated Gedaliah and other members of the court—throwing the dead bodies into a nearby cistern (see photo of a cistern of that day). Rather than kill every citizen, he also took captive a number of people who lived in Mizpah. Johanan, a man who had served Gedaliah faithfully, pursued Ishmael and recovered the prisoners. Ishmael, fearing for his life, fled to Ammon.

Through divine revelation, Jeremiah saw that this sequence of events could initiate the restoration of freedom for Judah (Jeremiah 42:10–12). He tried to convince the people to remain in the land and watch God restore their prosperity. The people, however, feared retribution from the king of Babylon and many fled to Egypt. Rather than find the freedom and safety they were seeking, the people who fled to Egypt died of plagues and other disasters. (Read the full story in 2 Kings 25:25 and Jeremiah 40–42.)

GEDALIAH IS ASSASSINATED

Ishmael flees to Gibeon with captives from Mizpah

Ishmael escapes to Ammon

Judeans flee to Egypt to escape retaliation by the Babylonians

0   10   20   30 mi

0   10   20   30   40 km

Mediterranean Sea

Tyre

Sea of Galilee

Megiddo

Beth-shan

Jordan River

Samaria

Mizpah

Gibeon

Jerusalem

Jericho

To AMMON

Dead Sea

Hebron

To EGYPT

Arad

N

Bethel

Ishmael assassinates the Babylonian governor Gedaliah and his officials

Mizpah

Michmash

Ramah   Geba

Gibeon

Gibeah

Anathoth

Johanan pursues Ishmael to Gibeon and recovers captives

Nob

Jerusalem

Bethlehem

0   2.5   5 mi

0   5 km

TYRE'S INTERNATIONAL TRADE

Tyre—a city to Israel's north—was well-known throughout the world for its trade. Tyre's seaport became a distribution point for its wood, purple dye, precious metals, and other natural resources. In addition to moving their own commercial goods, the Phoenicians who lived there built a prosperous economy buying and selling goods from around the world. (See photo for their sunset view over the Mediterranean.) The map indicates the breadth of the trading completed by those who lived in this seaport city. Ezekiel 27–28 recounts the vastness of the trade, listing the cities and items traded within their economy. The Bible recounts that Tyre was "situated at the gateway to the sea" and was the "merchant of people on many coasts" (Ezekiel 27:3).

Tyre's economic prosperity, however, could not purchase God's favor. Because of the people's sin, arrogance, and hard hearts, God pronounced judgment on the city. Ezekiel the prophet warned: "Because you think you are wise, as wise as a god, I [God] am going to bring foreigners against you, the most ruthless of nations; they will draw their swords against your beauty and wisdom and pierce your shining splendor. They will bring you down to the pit, and you will die a violent death in the heart of the seas" (Ezekiel 28:6–8).

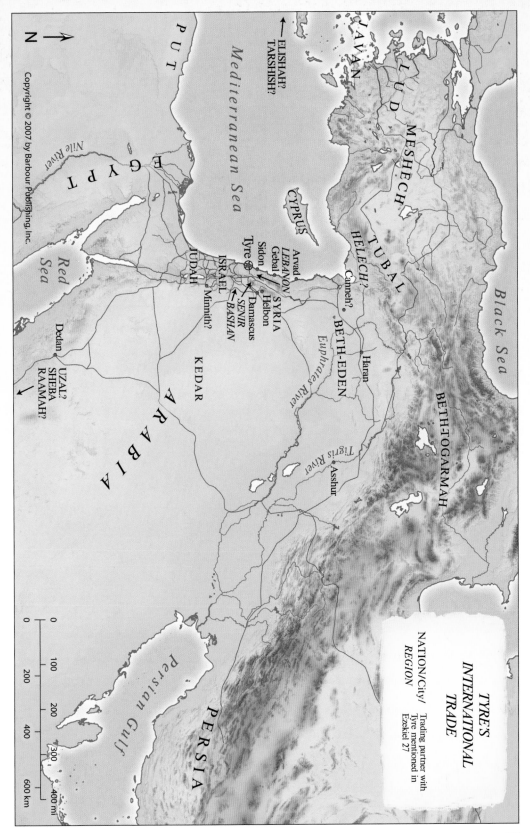

N →

ELISHAH?
TARSHISH?

Copyright © 2007 by Barbour Publishing, Inc.

Nile River

EGYPT

Mediterranean Sea

PUT

JAVAN

LUD

MESHECH

TUBAL

CYPRUS

HELECH?

Arvad
LEBANON
Gebal
Sidon
Tyre
JUDAH
ISRAEL
Minnith?
Helbon
Damascus
SENIR
BASHAN
SYRIA

Canneh?

BETH-EDEN

Haran

Euphrates River

BETH-TOGARMAH

Black Sea

Red Sea

Dedan
UZAL?
SHEBA
RAAMAH?

KEDAR

ARABIA

Tigris River
Asshur

PERSIA

Persian Gulf

0   100   200   400   600 km
0   100   200   300   400 mi

EZEKIEL'S VISION OF ISRAEL'S NEW BOUNDARIES

Ezekiel 47:13–48:35 records part of the prophet's apocalyptic vision. Because the temple Ezekiel envisioned has not yet been built, this vision seems to point to a future time.

At the time of his vision, Ezekiel's audience lived in exile. His message of a future home that was free from any potential defeat and threat of exile would have found an eager audience.

Ezekiel's temple stands in contrast to the other temples in Israel's history. Here are some of the important differences:

- There is no separate courtyard for gentiles.
- There is no reference to the temple artifacts used in traditional temple worship (for example, the table of showbread, lampstands, veil, laver, etc.).
- There is a miraculous, life-giving river that flows from the temple.

Many Christians draw connections between these differences and New Testament theology. For example, the New Testament includes all people equally into worship. Also, the river flowing from the temple in Ezekiel's vision is reminiscent of the river of life flowing from the throne of God in Revelation 22.

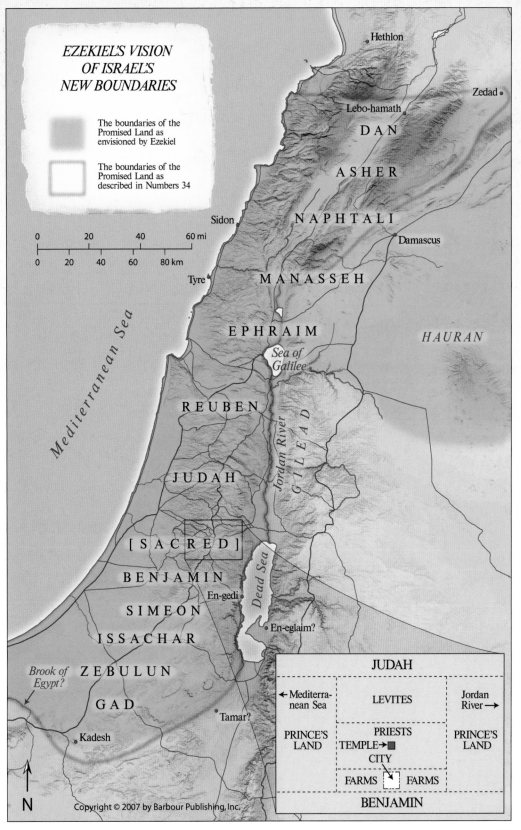

EZEKIEL'S VISION OF ISRAEL'S NEW BOUNDARIES

The boundaries of the Promised Land as envisioned by Ezekiel

The boundaries of the Promised Land as described in Numbers 34

0	20	40	60 mi

0	20	40	60	80 km

Hethlon

Zedad

Lebo-hamath

DAN

ASHER

NAPHTALI

Sidon

Damascus

Mediterranean Sea

MANASSEH

Tyre

EPHRAIM

Sea of Galilee

HAURAN

REUBEN

Jordan River

GILEAD

JUDAH

[S A C R E D]

Dead Sea

BENJAMIN

En-gedi

SIMEON

En-eglaim?

ISSACHAR

Brook of Egypt?

ZEBULUN

GAD

Tamar?

Kadesh

N

JUDAH		
← Mediterra-nean Sea	LEVITES	Jordan River →
PRINCE'S LAND	PRIESTS TEMPLE → ■ CITY	PRINCE'S LAND
	FARMS FARMS	
BENJAMIN		

THE GREEK EMPIRES

During Daniel's time of service under the Medes and the Persians, he saw a vision that greatly disturbed him (Daniel 8:27), perhaps because it spoke about the demise of the empire he served. In his vision, he saw the rise of the Greek Empire and its swift spread across the world (Daniel 8:5). That vision came true two hundred years after Daniel lived—when Alexander the Great conquered the world in twelve short years. (See photo of an ancient representation of Alexander the Great.)

Daniel's vision also foretold that the leader of Greece "at the height of his power. . .was broken off, and in its place four prominent horns grew up" (Daniel 8:8). As if following the script, Alexander the Great died at age thirty-two and his kingdom fell into a power struggle among his various generals. Eventually the borders came to resemble those shown on this map, with Cassander ruling in the east, Lysimachus ruling in the north by the Black Sea, Antigonus ruling in the center, Ptolemy ruling in the south, and Seleucus ruling in the east. Later Seleucus defeated Antigonus and claimed the area of Asia Minor for himself.

THE GREEK EMPIRES

- Empire of Alexander
- Empire of Lysimachus
- Empire of Antigonus
- Empire of Cassander
- Empire of Ptolemy
- Empire of Seleucus

N →

SAHARA DESERT

Mediterranean Sea

Cyrene

Alexandria

Memphis

Nile River

Thebes

Red Sea

ARABIAN DESERT

Paphos

Xanthus

Tyre

Jerusalem

Damascus

Babylon

Seleucia

Susa

Persepolis

Ecbatana

Issus

Euphrates River

Tigris River

Gaugamela

Arbela

Corinth

Athens

Miletus

Sardis

Cassandra

Lysimachia

Seuthopolis

Ister River

Black Sea

Caspian Sea

Aral Sea

Oxus River

Indus River

Marakanda

Bactra

Persian Gulf

0   200   400   600   800 km

0   200   400   600 mi

THE PTOLEMAIC AND THE SELEUCID EMPIRES (EARLY)

Daniel 11 unfolds another account of a prophetic vision seen by Daniel. Daniel 11:5 reads, "The king of the South will become strong, but one of his commanders will become even stronger than he and will rule his own kingdom with great power." This prophecy was fulfilled when Ptolemy's general, Seleucus, began to conquer the lands originally taken by Alexander and then divided by the other generals. Soon the Seleucid empire was established, which was greater than Ptolemy's territory in the south.

The photo on this page is of Acco/Ptolemais near sunset. Mt. Carmel is located in the background.

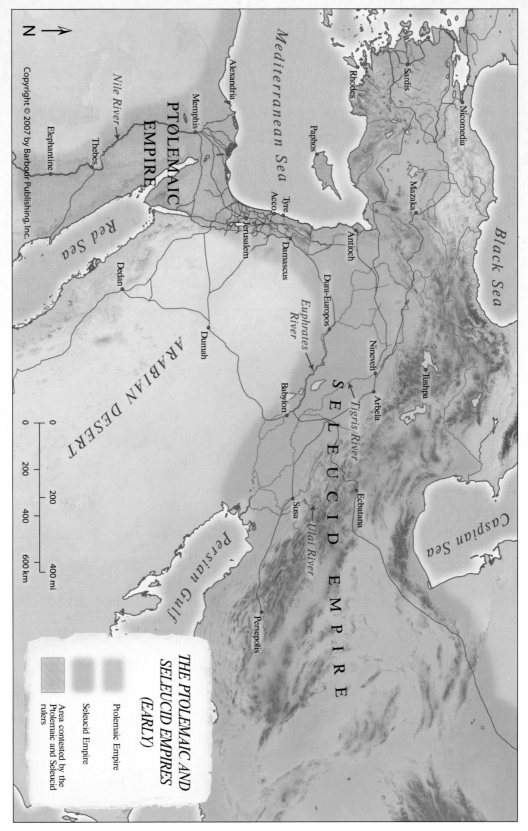

N →

Copyright © 2007 by Barbour Publishing, Inc.

Mediterranean Sea

Alexandria

Rhodes

Sardis

Nicomedia

Nile River

PTOLEMAIC
EMPIRE

Memphis

Paphos

Mazaka

Elephantine

Thebes

Black Sea

Acco
Tyre

Antioch

Red Sea

Jerusalem

Damascus

Dura-Europos

*Euphrates
River*

Nineveh

Tushpa

Dedan

S E L E U C I D   E M P I R E

Arbela

Tigris River

Ecbatana

A R A B I A N   D E S E R T

Dumah

Babylon

Susa

Ulai River

Caspian Sea

0   200   400   600 km

0   200   400 mi

Persian Gulf

Persepolis

THE PTOLEMAIC AND
SELEUCID EMPIRES
(EARLY)

Ptolemaic Empire

Seleucid Empire

Area contested by the
Ptolemaic and Seleucid
rulers

129

THE PTOLEMAIC AND THE SELEUCID EMPIRES (LATE)

Daniel 11:21–35 almost certainly predicts the rise of Antiochus Epiphanes. Further records of the events of this time are found in the extra-biblical books of the Maccabees.

Many Bible scholars also interpret Daniel 8:9–13 as a reference to Antiochus Epiphanes. History recounts that he ruled the land of Israel cruelly beginning in 167 BC. Because the Seleucid kingdom was beginning to wane (compare map on previous page with the map on this page), Antiochus tried to tighten his grip on his occupied territory by enforcing conformity and uniformity in religion and the Greek culture. Some of his escapades include:

- Sending twenty-two thousand soldiers to Jerusalem under the guise of a peace mission. However, they attacked the city on the Sabbath and slaughtered the people.
- He tried to Hellenize the Jewish people by ridding the land of temple worship.
- He burned copies of the Torah.
- He outlawed Jewish rites and customs such as circumcision.
- He erected an altar to Zeus on the temple mount, sacrificing a pig on it.

This final action is considered by many to be "the abomination that causes desolation" that is referenced in Daniel 8 and 11.

Within three years after this ultimate abomination, the Jewish people broke free from their oppressors and established an independent kingdom ruled by the Maccabeans. This kingdom lasted about one hundred years until Rome conquered the city in 63 BC. The photo above is of the traditional tombs of the Maccabees.

N →

Copyright © 2007 by Barbour Publishing, Inc.

THE NEAR EAST
DURING THE TIME
OF THE MACCABEES

THE PROPHETS OF
ISRAEL AND JUDAH

Many books in the Old Testament overview the reigns of the kings of the Northern and Southern Kingdoms. And while important, no recount of their history would be complete without remembering the prophets who served as God's mouthpieces during their reigns. Below are many of the major biblical prophets with references to the kings they served.

Key Prophets	The Kings They Primarily Served
Ahijah	Solomon and Jeroboam of the northern kingdom of Israel
Jehu	Baasha, Elah, and Zimri of Israel
Elijah	Ahab and Ahaziah of Israel
Elisha	Ahaziah, Jehu, and Jehoash of Israel
Jonah	Jeroboam II of Israel
Hosea	Jeroboam II (of Israel); Uzziah, Jotham, Ahaz, and Hezekiah (all of Judah)
Amos	Jeroboam II of Israel
Isaiah	Ahaz and Hezekiah of Judah
Micah	Jotham, Ahaz, and Hezekiah of Judah
Jeremiah	Josiah, Jehoahaz, Jehoiakim, Jehoiachin, and Zedekiah
Zephaniah	Josiah of Judah
Nahum	Josiah of Judah
Zechariah and Haggai	Served during reconstruction of temple after captivity
Malachi	Served after the people returned from exile
Prophets with unknown locations	
Joel	Uncertain
Obadiah	Uncertain
Habakkuk	Josiah of Judah
Prophets whose primary ministry occurred outside the promised land	
Ezekiel and Daniel	Primarily served while people were in exile

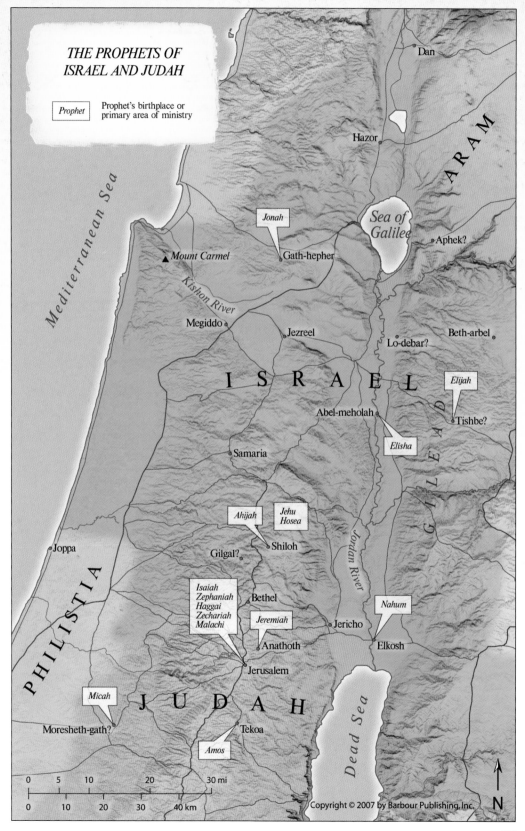

THE PROPHETS OF ISRAEL AND JUDAH

| *Prophet* | Prophet's birthplace or primary area of ministry |

Mediterranean Sea

Dan

Hazor

ARAM

Jonah

Sea of Galilee

Mount Carmel

Gath-hepher

Aphek?

Kishon River

Megiddo

Jezreel

Lo-debar?

Beth-arbel

ISRAEL

Elijah

Abel-meholah

Tishbe?

Elisha

Samaria

GILEAD

Ahijah

Jehu Hosea

Shiloh

Gilgal?

Jordan River

Joppa

Isaiah Zephaniah Haggai Zechariah Malachi

Bethel

Nahum

Jeremiah

Jericho

PHILISTIA

Anathoth

Elkosh

Jerusalem

Micah

JUDAH

Moresheth-gath?

Tekoa

Dead Sea

Amos

0   5   10   20   30 mi
0   10   20   30   40 km

Copyright © 2007 by Barbour Publishing, Inc.

N

THE NEW TESTAMENT

THE HOLY LAND IN THE TIME OF JESUS

Herod the Great ruled the land of Israel during the time of Jesus' birth. Called "King Herod," he had been appointed to his office by the Senate in Rome.

A paranoid ruler, Herod maintained power at times by violence. He executed one of his wives and murdered his sister's husband. When he felt threatened by his nephew, he marshaled his

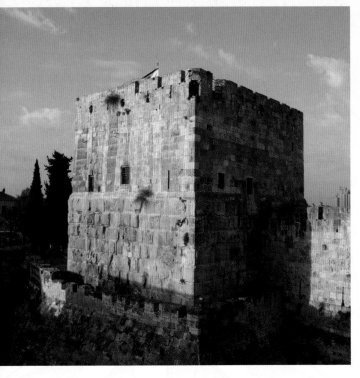

troops against him. He also married his own niece to secure his power. He also went as far as killing three of his own sons. With this background, it is not surprising that he issued a death sentence to a few baby boys living in the small town of Bethlehem—the town which was the purported home of a newly-born king (Luke 2).

While known for his use of strong force, Herod was also recognized as a master architect. Herod rebuilt the temple in Jerusalem, expanded the city walls, built a fortress at Masada, expanded the country's water supplies, and built a number of beautiful buildings throughout Israel that still stand (at least in part) today.

The photograph on this page shows walls and a tower known as the Citadel of David. This tower and portion of the wall were built by Herod the Great and would have been one of the views Jesus saw in Jerusalem.

At Herod's death, the country was divided between his three sons and each ruled over his own region (as indicated on the map).

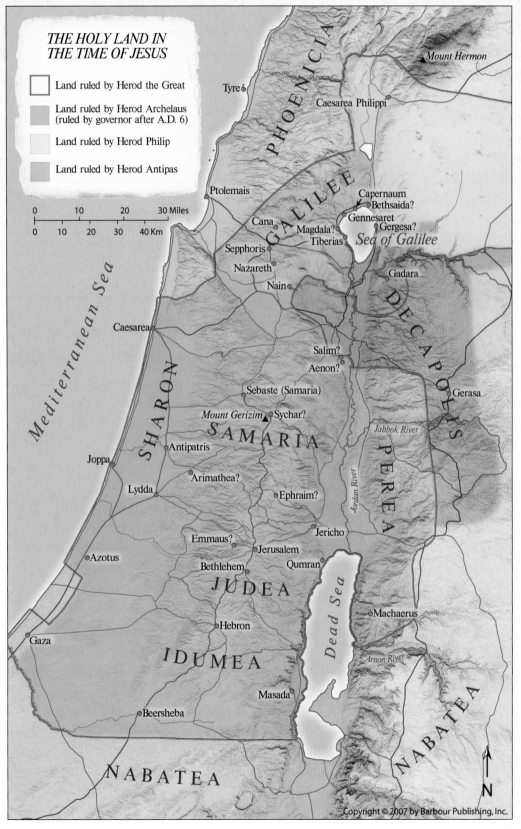

THE HOLY LAND IN
THE TIME OF JESUS

Land ruled by Herod the Great

Land ruled by Herod Archelaus
(ruled by governor after A.D. 6)

Land ruled by Herod Philip

Land ruled by Herod Antipas

0   10   20   30 Miles
0   10   20   30   40 Km

Mediterranean Sea

PHOENICIA

Mount Hermon

Tyre

Caesarea Philippi

GALILEE

Ptolemais

Cana

Capernaum
Bethsaida?
Gennesaret
Magdala?   Gergesa?
Tiberias   Sea of Galilee

Sepphoris

Nazareth

Nain

Gadara

DECAPOLIS

Caesarea

Salim?

Aenon?

Sebaste (Samaria)

Gerasa

Mount Gerizim   Sychar?

SAMARIA

Jabbok River

Antipatris

PEREA

Joppa

Jordan River

Arimathea?

Lydda

Ephraim?

Jericho

Emmaus?

Jerusalem

Azotus

Bethlehem

Qumran

JUDEA

Dead Sea

Machaerus

Hebron

IDUMEA

Gaza

Arnon River

NABATEA

Masada

Beersheba

NABATEA

N

JESUS' MINISTRY IN GALILEE AND BEYOND

Since the days that Jesus lived on earth, people of all faiths have claimed to control the traditional sites of key Bible events or locations that have been considered holy. In many cases, a church or other memorial was built over the location to preserve the ancient memory of Jesus or His disciples. For example, the photo on this page shows a modern church that was built over the home thought to be Peter's house. The photos reveal the care taken in building the church while leaving the remains of the house and later church buildings undisturbed.

Below are some of the events of Jesus' ministry that are listed on the map. Many of these locations are also marked with memorials and churches:

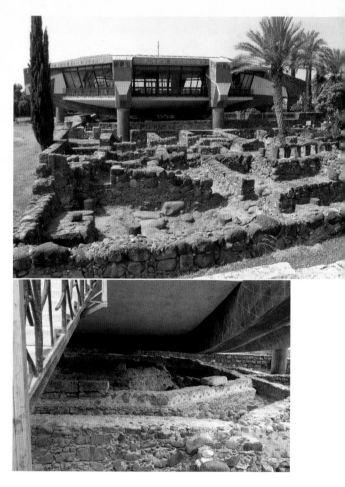

- Jesus heals the daughter of a Syrian Phoenician woman—Matthew 15; Mark 7
- The Transfiguration—Matthew 17; Mark 9; Luke 9
- Peter's confession—Matthew 16; Mark 8; Luke 9
- Jesus turns water into wine—John 2
- Feeding of the multitudes—Matthew 15; Mark 8; Luke 9; John 6
- Jesus casts demons into pigs—Matthew 8; Mark 5; Luke 8
- Jesus walks on water—Matthew 14; Mark 6; John 6
- Jesus raises a widow's son from the dead—Luke 7
- Jesus heals a man in the Decapolis—Mark 7
- Jesus heals ten lepers—Luke 17

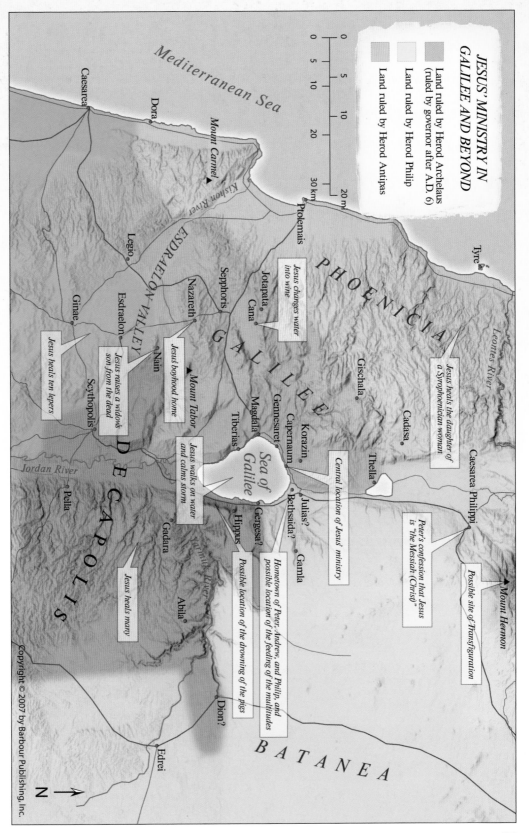

JESUS' MINISTRY IN
GALILEE AND BEYOND

Land ruled by Herod Archelaus
(ruled by governor after A.D. 6)

Land ruled by Herod Philip

Land ruled by Herod Antipas

Mediterranean Sea

Caesarea

Dora

Mount Carmel

Kishon River

Ptolemais

Tyre

PHOENICIA

Leontes River

Legio

ESDRAELON VALLEY

Sepphoris

Jotapata

Cana

Jesus changes water
into wine

Gischala

Cadasa

Jesus heals the daughter of
a Syrophoenician woman

Ginae

Esdraelon

Nazareth

Jesus' boyhood home

GALILEE

Jesus heals ten lepers

Nain

Jesus raises a widow's
son from the dead

Mount Tabor

Korazin

Capernaum

Gennesaret

Magdala

Thella

Caesarea Philippi

Scythopolis

Tiberias

Sea of
Galilee

Central location of Jesus' ministry

Peter's confession that Jesus
is "the Messiah (Christ)"

Possible site of Transfiguration

Mount Hermon

Jesus walks on water
and calms storm

Julias?

Bethsaida?

Gamla

Jordan River

Pella

D E C A P O L I S

Gadara

Hippus

Gergesa?

Hometown of Peter, Andrew, and Philip, and
possible location of the feeding of the multitudes

Yarmuk River

Jesus heals many

Abila

Possible location of the drowning of the pigs

Dion?

B A T A N E A

Edrei

N →

Copyright © 2007 by Barbour Publishing, Inc.

0 5 10 20 30 km
0 5 10 20 mi

THE LAST SUPPER

On the night before His death, Jesus and His disciples met in an upper room to eat the Passover meal together. This final meal has become known as the "Last Supper." The first photo below shows the room traditionally believed to be the location where Jesus and His disciples gathered for this meal.

Upon completing dinner, Jesus and His disciples went to the Garden of Gethsemane where Jesus spent considerable time in prayer (see bottom photo). Though the olive trees currently in this garden are very old—perhaps even fifteen hundred years old—they are not the same trees from Jesus' time. The Romans destroyed all of the trees around Jerusalem in AD 70.

The garden stands at the foot of the Mount of Olives, which is mentioned during the events of the holy week as well as in the story of King David. King David traveled to this mountain when Absalom led a revolt against him (2 Samuel 15:30).

Today the Mount of Olives is the site of many churches commemorating events in Jesus' life.

THE LAST SUPPER

——	Walls as they existed during Jesus' time
– – –	Walls begun shortly after Jesus' time
··········	Walls as they exist today
↓	Jesus' possible route to the garden of Gethsemane

0   1000   2000 ft
0   500 m

N →

Aqueducts

Wall begun and abandoned by Agrippa I c. A.D. 42

Golgotha (traditional location)

Towers Pool

Praetorium (former palace of Herod the Great)

Herod Antipas's Palace?

Antonia Fortress

Bethesda's Pools

Caiaphas's House?

Upper Room? (traditional location)

Pool of Siloam

Temple

Pool of Israel

HINNOM VALLEY

En-rogel

Gihon Spring

KIDRON VALLEY

Garden of Gethsemane

MOUNT OF OLIVES

Bethphage?

To Bethany →

JESUS' ARREST, TRIAL, AND CRUCIFIXION

Though the Jewish religious leaders wanted to put Jesus to death, they may not have had the civil authority to do so. Having found Jesus guilty in their own Jewish court, they also pursued a civil trial which would yield the death sentence they sought.

Although they recognized the Jewish leaders' motives, Herod Antipas and Pilate also knew that Jesus was a popular teacher among the people. This caused them to treat Jesus' trial with political gamesmanship—neither leader wanting to take the responsibility for condemning the popular teacher. And while they wanted to appease the Jewish leaders, they did not want to appear to be too heavily influenced by these men. Below is a list of events that occurred during Jesus' last days.

Event	Biblical Reference
The Last Supper	Matthew 26:20–30; Mark 14:17–26; Luke 22:14–38; John 13–14
Jesus arrested	Matthew 26:47–56; Mark 14:43–52; Luke 22:47–53; John 18:1–12
Jesus found guilty by Jewish leaders	Matthew 27:1–2; Mark 15:1; Luke 22:66–71
Jesus before Pilate for first trial	Matthew 27:11–14; Mark 15:2–5; Luke 23:1–5; John 18:28–37
Pilate defers Jesus' case to Herod Antipas	Luke 23:6–12
Herod returns Jesus to Pilate	Luke 23:11
Pilate sentences Jesus to death	Matthew 27:26; Mark 15:15; Luke 23:23–24; John 19:16
Jesus crucified	Matthew 27:32–34; Mark 15:21–25; Luke 23:26–34; John 19:16–24
Jesus buried in tomb of Joseph of Arimathea	Matthew 27:57–61; Mark 15:42–47; Luke 23:50–56; John 19:38–42
Jesus' resurrection	Matthew 28:1–3, Mark 16:1–8, Luke 24:1–12, John 20:1–9

JESUS ARREST, TRIAL,
AND CRUCIFIXION

——— Walls as they existed
during Jesus' time

·········· Walls as they exist
today

⟶ Jesus is arrested, tried,
and crucified

Bethesda's Pools

Pool of Israel

Antonia
Fortress

Garden of
Gethsemane

Sheep Gate?

Temple

Golgotha
(traditional
location)

Towers
Pool

Beautiful
Gate

Herod
Antipas's
Palace?

Pinnacle
(traditional
location)

Praetorium
(former palace of
Herod the Great)

KIDRON VALLEY

UPPER CITY

LOWER CITY

Gihon Spring

Caiaphas's House?

Upper Room?
(traditional
location)

Pool of
Siloam

HINNOM VALLEY

N

En-rogel

Copyright © 2007 by Barbour Publishing, Inc.

THE JOURNEY TO EMMAUS

Luke 24:13–32 records the story of Jesus' post-resurrection appearance to two disciples as they walked to Emmaus. The story takes place just after several of Jesus' followers had visited His tomb and found it empty. Not only was the tomb empty, but some of the women said angels explained the empty tomb by reminding them that Jesus had said He would rise again on the third day. One of the women even claimed to have encountered Jesus personally.

It's clear by the demeanor of these two followers that either they were unsure about the validity of these reports or unsure about their meaning. Either way, they were disappointed that their original expectations for Jesus had not been met.

Along the way, Jesus joined them. His true identity was hidden from them either by physical changes to His body or by divine intervention. As they walked, Jesus explained to them the important purposes behind the crucifixion and resurrection. Just when Jesus opened their eyes and allowed them to recognize the identity of their traveling companion, He disappeared from their sight. Fueled by the emotion of their encounter, they risked travel by night to tell the disciples in Jerusalem what they had seen and learned.

Below is a list of many of the post-resurrection appearances of Jesus as they are recorded in the New Testament.

Appearance	Biblical Reference
Jesus appears to Mary at the tomb.	Matthew 28:9–10; Mark 16:9; John 20:10–17
Jesus appears (twice) to the disciples in a locked room.	Luke 24:36–48; John 20:19–29
Jesus appears to two followers on the road to Emmaus.	Mark 16:12–13; Luke 24:13–32
Jesus appears to seven of His disciples—including Peter—beside the Sea of Galilee.	John 21:1–23
Jesus appears to the eleven disciples and gives them the "Great Commission."	Matthew 28:16–20; Mark 16:18
Jesus appears to Peter.	Luke 24:34; 1 Corinthians 15:5
Jesus appears to 500 people at once.	1 Corinthians 15:6
Jesus appears to James.	1 Corinthians 15:7
Jesus ascends to heaven in the presence of many.	Mark 16:19–20; Luke 24:50–51; Acts 1:4–9
Jesus appears to Paul.	Acts 9:1–9; 1 Corinthians 15:8

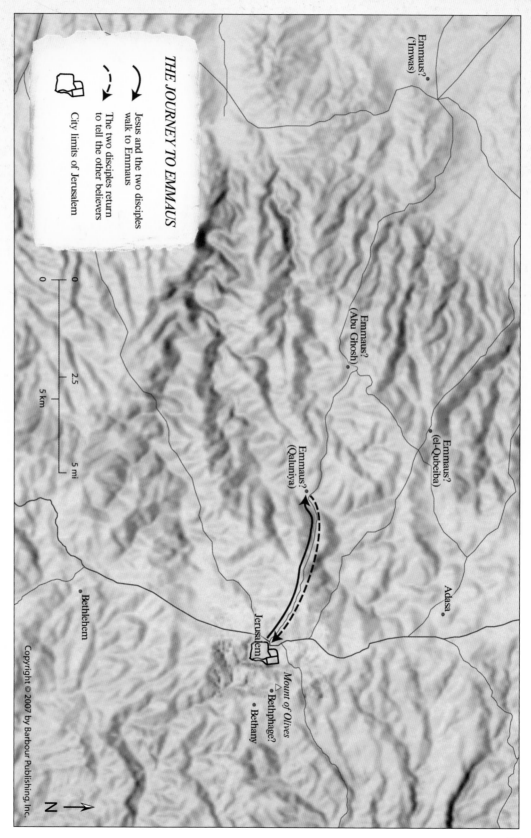

THE JOURNEY TO EMMAUS

Jesus and the two disciples walk to Emmaus

The two disciples return to tell the other believers

City limits of Jerusalem

Emmaus? ('Imwas)

Emmaus? (Abu Ghosh)

Emmaus? (el-Qubeiba)

Emmaus? (Qaluniya)

Adasa

Jerusalem

Mount of Olives
Bethphage?
Bethany

Bethlehem

0

2.5

5 km

5 mi

N →

THE NATIONS AT PENTECOST

Pentecost, or the time of the "Harvest Offering," was one of the seven great feasts celebrated by the Jewish people (see Leviticus 23:15–22). With an international crowd on hand for the festival, God established the church by supernaturally em-powering His disciples with the Holy Spirit. Acts 2 describes this incredible event and delineates the many nations represented in the crowd—each one hearing the gospel preached in their own native language (Acts 2:6–11). The map, showing the nations listed in Acts in red type, indicates the variety of languages represented by the thousands that attended this gathering.

This event marks a turning point in the New Testament: The first half of the New Testament records the life of Jesus, His death, and His resurrection. The outpouring of the Holy Spirit at Pentecost shifts the focus from the earthly life of Christ to the establishment of His church. Below is a timeline of major events that occurred in the New Testament:

4 BC or 5 BC	The birth of Jesus
AD 26–30	The public ministry of Jesus
AD 26	The ministry of John the Baptist begins
AD 30	The death and resurrection of Jesus
AD 33	The conversion of Saul of Tarsus
AD 47–48	Paul's first missionary journey (see map on page 154)
AD 50–52	Paul's second missionary journey (see map on page 156)
AD 53–57	Paul's final missionary journey (see map on page 158)

THE NATIONS
AT PENTECOST

PLACE   Location represented
at Pentecost according
to Acts 2

Roman Empire

Parthian Empire

0   100   200   300   400 mi
0   200   400   600 km

Copyright © 2007 by Barbour Publishing, Inc.

Peter preaches at the
Temple at Pentecost

Mediterranean Sea

Adriatic Sea

Black Sea

Caspian Sea

Red Sea

Persian Gulf

Rome

ITALY

Syracuse

Thessalonica

GREECE

Athens

CRETE

Ephesus

ASIA

PHRYGIA

PAMPHYLIA

Nicomedia

CAPPADOCIA

PONTUS

Artaxata

MEDIA

Ecbatana

PARTHIA

Susa

ELAM

Ctesiphon

MESOPOTAMIA

Melitene

Dura-Europos

Antioch

SYRIA

Jerusalem

JUDEA

ARABIA

ARABIAN
DESERT

Tema

Cyrene

LIBYA

Alexandria

EGYPT

Thebes

N →

PHILIP'S MINISTRY

Acts 8 records many events from the ministry of Philip, one of the original twelve disciples of Jesus. Driven from Jerusalem by the persecution against Christians, Philip preached the gospel in Samaria before returning to Jerusalem—the home base of the church. Once back in the city, God instructed Philip to travel to Gaza. Along the way, Philip met an official from the court of the Ethiopian queen. This man was reading from the Hebrew scriptures and trying to determine their meaning.

Philip interpreted the scriptures for him and told him about Jesus. Acts 8:38 records that the man put his faith in Christ, was baptized, and returned to Ethiopia. The Acts account then recounts how Philip was miraculously transported to the town of Azotus, where he continued preaching until he reached Caesarea.

The town of Caesarea was the Roman administrative center of the region and had been an important center for Herod the Great's building projects. A port city that would see many travelers, this town became an important showpiece for Herod and his projects. One of his most lasting structures is called the Hippodrome (see photo). This structure provided a powerful impression for travelers as they entered the city. With a seating capacity of thousands, this stadium was 250 yards long and 90 yards across. According to the Jewish historian Josephus, Herod Agrippa died while near this venue. Acts records the event this way: "Herod, wearing his royal robes, sat on his throne and delivered a public address to the people. They shouted, 'This is the voice of a god, not of a man.' Immediately, because Herod did not give praise to God, an angel of the Lord struck him down, and he was eaten by worms and died" (Acts 12:21–23).

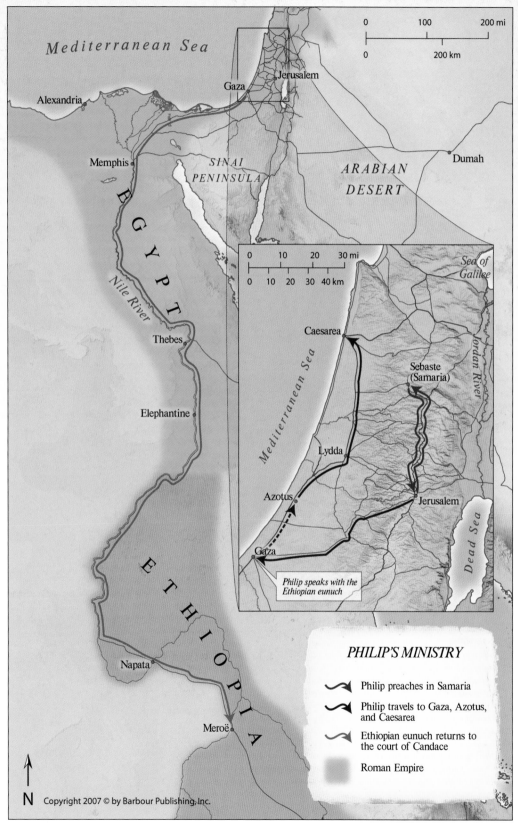

Mediterranean Sea

Gaza

Jerusalem

Alexandria

Memphis

Dumah

SINAI
PENINSULA

ARABIAN
DESERT

E G Y P T

Nile River

Thebes

Elephantine

0   10   20   30 mi

0   10   20   30   40 km

Sea of
Galilee

Caesarea

Sebaste
(Samaria)

Jordan River

Lydda

Mediterranean Sea

Azotus

Jerusalem

Gaza

Dead Sea

*Philip speaks with the
Ethiopian eunuch*

E T H I O P I A

Napata

Meroë

PHILIP'S MINISTRY

Philip preaches in Samaria

Philip travels to Gaza, Azotus,
and Caesarea

Ethiopian eunuch returns to
the court of Candace

Roman Empire

N

SAUL'S CONVERSION AND EARLY TRAVELS

It's difficult to imagine the story of the early church without Paul (originally known as Saul). This giant of Christian faith and history seems to be ever-present in the second half of the New Testament. The verses in Acts 9 and beyond read so matter-of-factly that it appears that Paul's public ministry began at the moment he converted to Christianity. The reality, however, is that Paul spent several years in preparation before becoming a traveling evangelist and prominent New Testament figure. Below is a list of events that occurred during Paul's early years as a Christian.

- The Jewish leaders give Paul permission to arrest Christians. Jesus appears to Paul during his journey to Damascus, leaving him blinded (Acts 9:1–9).
- Ananias prays for Paul and God restores his sight (Acts 9:17–18).
- Paul spends time in Arabia growing in his new-found faith (Galatians 1:17). While we don't know how long he was in Arabia, we do know that it was three years before Paul returned to Jerusalem (Galatians 1:18).
- With the help of Barnabas, Paul joins the church in Jerusalem (Acts 9:27).
- His life threatened, Paul escapes to Caesarea where he boards a ship to his home city of Tarsus (Acts 9:30).
- Paul lives in Tarsus for five or six years until Barnabas recruits him to travel to Antioch (Acts 11:25–26).

The city of Tarsus was an important Roman city with a rich heritage. The photo on this page shows the Cleopatra Gate which stands at the west end of Tarsus; this is where Anthony and Cleopatra marched into the city in 41 BC. The restoration process has kept the original structure intact but has covered much of the original stone facing.

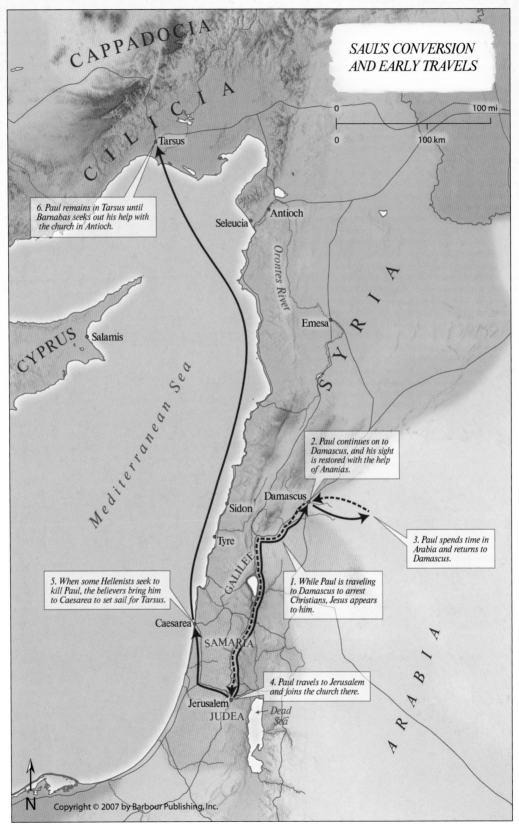

SAUL'S CONVERSION
AND EARLY TRAVELS

CAPPADOCIA

C I L I C I A

Tarsus

6. Paul remains in Tarsus until
Barnabas seeks out his help with
the church in Antioch.

Seleucia

Antioch

Orontes River

S Y R I A

CYPRUS

Salamis

Emesa

Mediterranean Sea

Damascus

2. Paul continues on to
Damascus, and his sight
is restored with the help
of Ananias.

Sidon

3. Paul spends time in
Arabia and returns to
Damascus.

Tyre

GALILEE

5. When some Hellenists seek to
kill Paul, the believers bring him
to Caesarea to set sail for Tarsus.

1. While Paul is traveling
to Damascus to arrest
Christians, Jesus appears
to him.

Caesarea

SAMARIA

A R A B I A

4. Paul travels to Jerusalem
and joins the church there.

Jerusalem
JUDEA

Dead
Sea

N

Copyright © 2007 by Barbour Publishing, Inc.

PETER'S EARLY MINISTRY AND THE KINGDOM OF AGRIPPA I

Though a central figure in the early church in Jerusalem (Acts 1–12), Peter's ministry took him beyond the limits of the church's headquarters. Acts 9–10 records his visits to other cities and the boldness with which he shared the gospel message. These chapters capture three significant events in the ministry of Peter and of the early church:

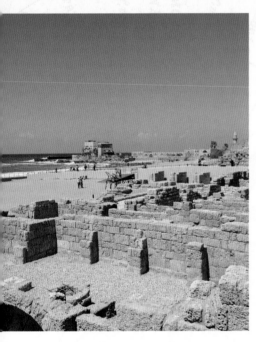

- Peter heals a paralyzed man named Aeneas (Acts 9:33).
- Peter raises Dorcas from the dead in Joppa (Acts 9:40).
- Peter shares the gospel with Cornelius in Caesarea (Acts 10). Through this event with Cornelius, God brought Peter and the rest of the disciples to the realization that Gentiles were also to be welcomed as members of God's family.

Caesarea was an important city to Herod the Great (see page 148). As the access point to his kingdom for those coming from Rome, Herod made sure this city would impress visitors. As part of his building plan, Herod developed a forty-acre harbor, which accommodated as many as three hundred ships. These building projects made Caesarea a well-traveled city and an important center for world trade and communication.

Many years after Cornelius's conversion, the apostle Paul was a prisoner in Caesarea (Acts 26). Approximately 125 years later, this city became the home of Origen, a Christian philosopher who lived between AD 185 and 254.

Through the teachings of Peter, Paul, and later Origen, Caesarea became both a symbolic and strategic location for the spread of the Christian faith.

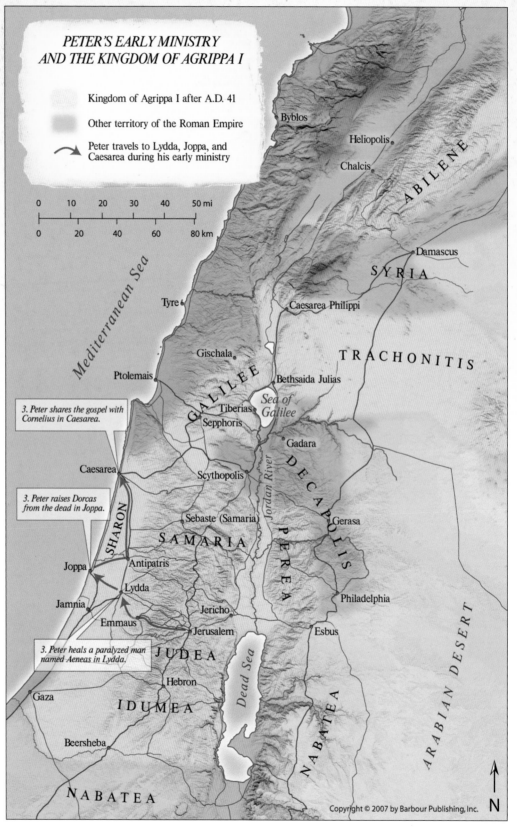

PETER'S EARLY MINISTRY
AND THE KINGDOM OF AGRIPPA I

Kingdom of Agrippa I after A.D. 41

Other territory of the Roman Empire

Peter travels to Lydda, Joppa, and
Caesarea during his early ministry

0   10   20   30   40   50 mi

0   20   40   60   80 km

Byblos

Heliopolis

Chalcis

ABILENE

Damascus

SYRIA

Mediterranean Sea

Tyre

Caesarea Philippi

TRACHONITIS

Gischala

Ptolemais

GALILEE

Bethsaida Julias

3. Peter shares the gospel with
Cornelius in Caesarea.

Tiberias

Sea of
Galilee

Sepphoris

Gadara

Caesarea

Scythopolis

DECAPOLIS

Jordan River

PEREA

3. Peter raises Dorcas
from the dead in Joppa.

SHARON

Sebaste (Samaria)

Gerasa

SAMARIA

Joppa

Antipatris

Philadelphia

Lydda

Jamnia

Jericho

Emmaus

Jerusalem

Esbus

3. Peter heals a paralyzed man
named Aeneas in Lydda.

JUDEA

Dead Sea

NABATEA

ARABIAN DESERT

Hebron

Gaza

IDUMEA

Beersheba

NABATEA

N

PAUL'S FIRST MISSIONARY JOURNEY

When the church in Antioch decided to send a missionary team to preach Christ throughout other parts of the world, Barnabas went to Tarsus to recruit Paul for the work (Acts 11:25–26). Paul joined Barnabas in Antioch, and the two men (along with John Mark) traveled by ship on what has become known as Paul's first missionary journey. This trip most likely occurred in AD 47–48 and is chronicled in Acts 13–14.

The outbound portion of the trip focused on preaching Christ to the people within each of these cities and introducing them to Christianity. The inbound portion of the trip retraced the missionaries' steps in order to visit and encourage those who had become Christians during the first portion of their journey.

Some of the significant events that occurred during the first missionary journey include:

- Sergius Paulus, the governor of Cyprus, becomes a Christian (Acts 13:7).
- John Mark leaves Paul and Barnabas at Perga (Acts 13:13).
- Paul and Barnabas preach the gospel to the Gentiles in Pisidian Antioch (Acts 13:14).
- Paul is stoned in Lystra (Acts 14:19).

The photograph of the catacombs captures the influence of Christianity on the island of Cyprus. Though originally built as tombs, these underground rooms and tunnels were later converted to a Christian church.

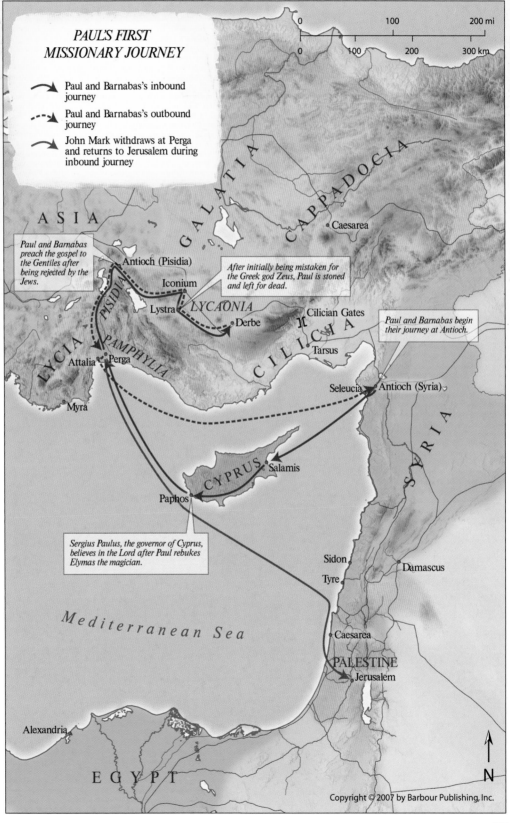

PAUL'S FIRST MISSIONARY JOURNEY

- Paul and Barnabas's inbound journey
- Paul and Barnabas's outbound journey
- John Mark withdraws at Perga and returns to Jerusalem during inbound journey

0   100   200 mi
0 100 200 300 km

ASIA

GALATIA

CAPPADOCIA

Caesarea

Paul and Barnabas preach the gospel to the Gentiles after being rejected by the Jews.

Antioch (Pisidia)

Iconium

PISIDIA

Lystra

LYCAONIA

Derbe

After initially being mistaken for the Greek god Zeus, Paul is stoned and left for dead.

Cilician Gates

CILICIA

Tarsus

Paul and Barnabas begin their journey at Antioch.

LYCIA

PAMPHYLIA

Attalia Perga

Myra

Seleucia

Antioch (Syria)

SYRIA

CYPRUS

Salamis

Paphos

Sergius Paulus, the governor of Cyprus, believes in the Lord after Paul rebukes Elymas the magician.

Sidon

Tyre

Damascus

Mediterranean Sea

Caesarea

PALESTINE

Jerusalem

Alexandria

EGYPT

N

Copyright © 2007 by Barbour Publishing, Inc.

PAUL'S SECOND MISSIONARY JOURNEY

Paul's second missionary journey allowed him to revisit several churches he had established while on his way to Greece. This journey took place between AD 50 and 52 and is recorded in Acts 15–18.

While in Antioch preparing for their journey, Paul and Barnabas had a strong disagreement about the role of John Mark. Even though the young man had previously deserted them (Acts 13:13), Barnabas wanted to include him on this new trip—an idea Paul strongly opposed. The disagreement became so severe that Paul and Barnabas parted ways. Barnabas took John Mark and traveled to Cyprus, while Paul teamed up with Silas and continued his own journey west (Acts 15:39–41).

Early on, Paul spent time in Lystra. There he met Timothy who joined the missionary team for the rest of the journey (Acts 16:1–3). Their longest stay was in Corinth (about eighteen months), where they preached the gospel and strengthened Christians in their faith.

This region of Greece was steeped in religion. For example, the people of Athens wanted to ensure the favor of any deity they may have overlooked, so they dedicated an altar to "an unknown God" (Acts 17:23). Corinth itself housed a Temple of Apollo (see photo). A densely populated area, the city of Corinth probably had about eight hundred thousand residents during Paul's visit.

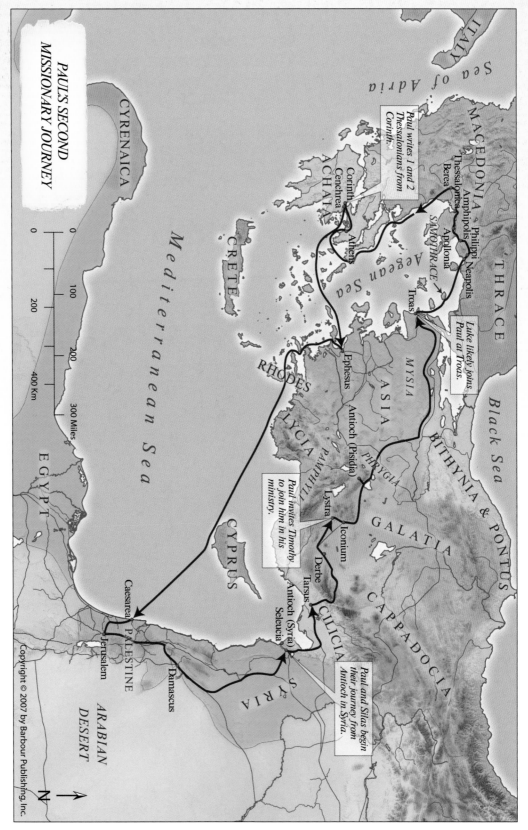

PAUL'S SECOND MISSIONARY JOURNEY

Paul writes 1 and 2 Thessalonians from Corinth.

Luke likely joins Paul at Troas.

Paul invites Timothy to join him in his ministry.

Paul and Silas begin their journey from Antioch in Syria.

Copyright © 2007 by Barbour Publishing, Inc.

157

PAUL'S THIRD MISSIONARY JOURNEY

Paul's third missionary journey began nearly as soon as his second journey ended. This journey, which occurred between AD 52 or 53 and AD 56 or 57, is recorded in Acts 18–21. Beginning in Antioch, this trip allowed Paul to retrace his steps to regions and cities he had already visited in order to preach the gospel to new listeners and bolster the faith of those already converted. The trip ended in Jerusalem with his arrest and Roman imprisonment.

Paul's longest stop during this trip was in the city of Ephesus, where he spent three years. There Paul met Apollos, spent time teaching him, and then sent him to minister to the church in Corinth.

Ephesus was a very advanced city in its day. Spiritually, the city was famous for its temple of Artemis—now known as one of the seven wonders of the world. As a place of worship, this ancient temple was four times the size of the Parthenon of Athens. Culturally, they could boast of sophisticated technology, such as a public latrine system (see photo). They built the latrine over a channel of moving water, which moved the waste out of the city. Socially, the culture encouraged indulgence in sexual promiscuity—with at least one large brothel that ran a successful business.

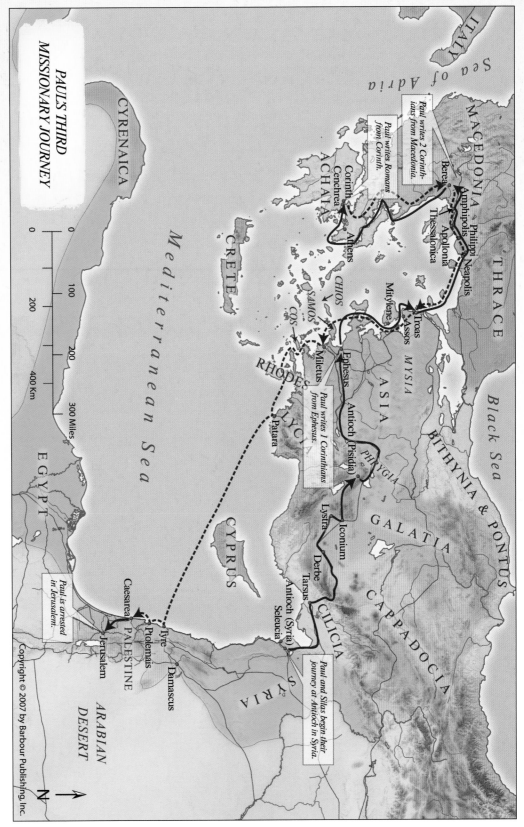

PAUL'S THIRD
MISSIONARY JOURNEY

Paul writes 2 Corinth-
ians from Macedonia.

Paul writes Romans
from Corinth.

Paul writes 1 Corinthians
from Ephesus.

Paul is arrested
in Jerusalem.

Paul and Silas begin their
journey at Antioch in Syria.

CYRENAICA

CRETE

Mediterranean Sea

ITALY

Sea of Adria

MACEDONIA

Berea
Corinth
Cenchrea
Athens
Amphipolis
Apollonia
Thessalonica
Philippi
Neapolis

ACHAIA

THRACE

Black Sea

CHIOS

SAMOS

COS

RHODES

LYCIA

Patara

Mitylene
Troas
Assos

MYSIA

ASIA

BITHYNIA & PONTUS

Miletus
Ephesus
Antioch (Pisidia)

PHRYGIA

GALATIA

Lystra
Iconium
Derbe
Tarsus
Antioch (Syria)
Seleucia

CAPPADOCIA

CILICIA

CYPRUS

EGYPT

Caesarea
Ptolemais
Tyre
Damascus
Jerusalem

PALESTINE

SYRIA

ARABIAN
DESERT

0
0
100
200
200
400 Km
300 Miles

N

PAUL'S VOYAGE TO ROME

Certain Jewish leaders went to great lengths to stir up trouble for Paul. As they had done with Jesus, they hoped to use political pressure on the Roman leaders to have Paul executed or put in a position where he could be ambushed and killed en route to his trial (Acts 25:3). Perhaps because of his knowledge of their tendencies and plans, Paul appealed his case to Caesar himself—as was his right as a Roman citizen: "If, however, I am guilty of doing anything deserving death, I do not refuse

to die. But if the charges brought against me by these Jews are not true, no one has the right to hand me over to them. I appeal to Caesar!" (Acts 25:11).

So the authorities turned Paul over to a Roman guard for escort to Rome where he would face charges in the Emperor's court.

While sailing to Rome, the ship encountered strong winds and was eventually wrecked on the Island of Malta. (See photo of traditional location in what is now know as St. Paul's Bay.)

Once in Rome, Paul lived under house arrest and wrote letters to the churches he had visited many times during his missionary journeys.

PAUL'S VOYAGE TO ROME

Copyright © 2007 by Barbour Publishing, Inc.

THE ROMAN EMPIRE IN THE TIME OF PAUL

At the peak of its expansion, Rome controlled 2.3 million square miles of land that encompassed the Mediterranean Sea. To a certain degree, Rome brought peace to its world and built many structures that still exist today (see photo of Roman Colosseum). And while the conquered people—especially the Jewish people in Palestine—resented Roman occupation, Paul and the early Christians benefited from the empire in the following ways:

- Initial Roman tolerance for Christianity trumped the Jewish leaders' persecution. For example, when the Jewish leaders wanted to put Paul to death, Rome's laws allowed Paul an appeal to Caesar. Once in Rome, Paul preached the gospel, helped establish the local church, and wrote letters that became part of the New Testament.

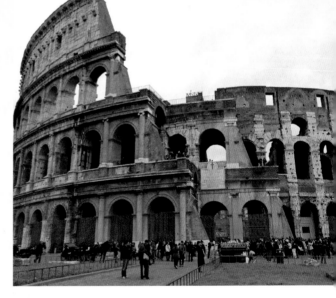

- Roman infrastructure also aided early Christians. The Roman roads and civil institutions allowed Christians to travel the Roman world quickly and without hindrance.
- The Roman peace (or Pax Romana) that occurred between 27 BC and AD 180 meant that the empire was not usually at war. Christians traveled freely by land and sea without major hindrances. The dense populations of many cities provided a large audience for the Christian message.
- A common language also united the western world. While many people groups held on to their local languages, Koine Greek became a universally understood language. The New Testament books were distributed in a common language, allowing a quick dissemination of the apostle's teaching.
- While the Roman government eventually turned hostile toward Christians—from the time of Nero (AD 54) until Constantine (AD 313)—the early decades of peace allowed orthodox Christianity to spread with little hindrance.

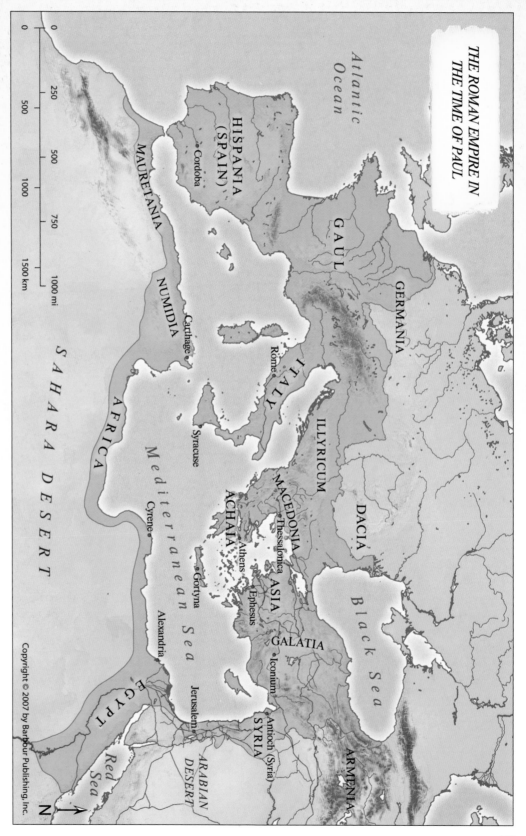

THE ROMAN EMPIRE IN
THE TIME OF PAUL

Atlantic
Ocean

HISPANIA
(SPAIN)

Cordoba

GAUL

GERMANIA

MAURETANIA

NUMIDIA

Carthage

AFRICA

S A H A R A   D E S E R T

ITALY

Rome

Syracuse

M e d i t e r r a n e a n   S e a

Cyrene

ILLYRICUM

MACEDONIA

Thessalonica

ACHAIA

Athens

Gortyna

Ephesus

ASIA

DACIA

Black Sea

GALATIA

Iconium

EGYPT

Alexandria

Jerusalem

Antioch (Syria)

SYRIA

ARMENIA

ARABIAN
DESERT

Red
Sea

N

0   250   500   750   1000 mi
0   500   1000   1500 Km

THE CHURCHES OF REVELATION

Because of their dense population and key location along Roman routes, the seven cities mentioned in the book of Revelation became strategic during the spread of Christianity. While several of these cities were likely visited by Paul or other disciples, the apostle John wrote to them in order to wake them from the complacency they had fallen into. Below are the seven churches he mentions.

City	Biblical Reference	What We Know about Them
Ephesus	Rev. 2:1–7	John corrected them for leaving their first love. See more detailed description on page 158.
Smyrna	Rev. 2:8–11	This church suffered persecution and poverty. This city was known for its commerce and strategic harbors.
Pergamum	Rev. 2:12–17	This city played a vital role in Roman commerce and travel. A very worldly city, John reprimanded them for mixing accepted cultural practices into the doctrines of the church.
Thyatira	Rev. 2:18–29	This church was lured away from the gospel message by a prophetess reminiscent of the evil Jezebel.
Sardis	Rev. 3:1–6	The church in this city had been lulled to sleep by worldly influences. This city, known for its hedonistic temples and bath houses, seemed to have tempted the Christians away from their devotion for Christ.
Philadelphia	Rev. 3:7–13	John commended this church for waiting patiently for Jesus' return. Philadephia was a very religious city that contained many temples and places of worship.
Laodicea	Rev. 3:14–22	Laodicea was located near hot and cold springs, which would have made John's rebuke for being "lukewarm" very personal.

John wrote this letter while exiled on the island of Patmos (see photo). According to church tradition, John lived out his final years on this island. And while he had become elderly, tradition says that John was released in AD 96 upon the death of Emperor Domitian and the accession of the Emperor Nerva.

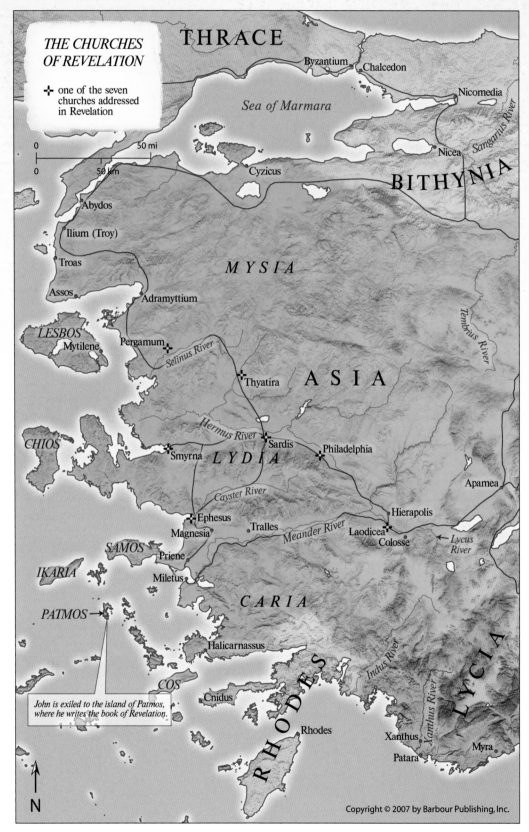

THE CHURCHES
OF REVELATION

✛ one of the seven
churches addressed
in Revelation

0   50 mi
0   50 km

THRACE

Byzantium
Chalcedon

Nicomedia

Sea of Marmara

Sangarius River

Cyzicus

Nicea

BITHYNIA

Abydos

Ilium (Troy)

Troas

MYSIA

Assos

Adramyttium

Tembrius River

LESBOS
Mytilene

Pergamum ✛

Selinus River

✛ Thyatira

ASIA

Hermus River

CHIOS

✛ Sardis

Philadelphia ✛

Smyrna ✛

LYDIA

Apamea

Cayster River

Hierapolis

Ephesus ✛

Tralles

Meander River

Laodicea

Magnesia

Colosse

Lycus
River

SAMOS

Priene

IKARIA

Miletus

CARIA

PATMOS →

Indus River

Xanthus River

LYCIA

Halicarnassus

COS

John is exiled to the island of Patmos,
where he writes the book of Revelation.

Cnidus

RHODES

Rhodes

Xanthus

Myra

Patara

Copyright © 2007 by Barbour Publishing, Inc.

ADDITIONAL INFORMATION:

Enemies of Israel

The people of Israel have had many enemies throughout their history. Here are some of the hostile neighbors we read about throughout biblical history.

AMALEKITES—These people were descendants of Esau and lived on the southern border of Israel near the desert region of Paran. They battled the people of Israel from the time of Moses (Exodus 17), through the time of the judges (Judges 6). King Saul and King David ultimately vanquished them (1 Samuel 15, 27, 30; 2 Samuel 8).

AMMONITES—The people of Ammon were descendants of Abraham's nephew Lot. As relatives of God's people, God had instructed the people of Israel not to harm them during their conquest of Canaan (Deuteronomy 2:19). And since these people lived east of the Jordan River, they were left mostly undisturbed. During the time of the judges, however, the Ammonites raided Israel. Jephthah became a judge and defeated the Ammonites (Judges 11).

AMORITES—The Amorites lived to the south of Israel and worshiped Baal and Asherah, which were common gods in the region. Saul defeated the Amorites in 2 Samuel 21:2.

ASSYRIANS—The ten tribes of the Northern Kingdom were conquered and removed from the land by Assyria (2 Kings 17), which ruled much of the region between 934 and 612 BC. Assyria was known for being the cruelest and most vicious empire in the ancient world, inventing creative, painful ways to kill those who rebelled against them.

BABYLONIANS—In the mid-600s BC, Babylon rose to power by defeating the Assyrians. Babylon's King Nebuchadnezzar defeated the southern kingdom of Israel (2 Chronicles 36) and took Daniel captive (Daniel 1). While in captivity, Daniel became a high-ranking advisor to the king of Babylon and later to the Medes and Persians who conquered the Babylonians (Daniel 6:28).

CANAANITES—The term *Canaanites* referred to different tribes and peoples living in the land of Canaan during the time of Joshua (Joshua 3, 7, 9, 17). Generally, the people of the land worshiped Baal and Asherah. When Israel didn't conquer and remove these people completely as God had commanded, their influence in the areas of religion and culture began to have a negative influence on the spiritual life of God's people.

EDOMITES—These descendants of Esau lived to the southeast of Israel and on the opposite side of the Dead Sea. While Moses was leading the people to the promised land, the king of Edom refused to allow the Hebrews to pass through their land (Numbers 20). King David severely defeated the Edomites so that they never again became a serious threat to the people (2 Samuel 8). Edom existed in a vassal relationship with the Southern Kingdom for many years, occasionally securing independence.

EGYPTIANS—Once Israel received its independence from Pharaoh, the people migrated and settled in the land of Israel. At times the nations of Israel and Egypt lived peacefully together. At other times, hostilities arose—most notably when Pharaoh Neco brought his army through the region (2 Kings 23; 2 Chronicles 35).

GREEKS—The era of Israel's Northern and Southern Kingdoms was over by the time Greece rose to power (as prophesied in Daniel 8 and 10). The people of the Southern Kingdom were already subject to the Medes when Alexander the Great's army swept through the region. It was because of the Greek influence that people in the Mediterranean region spoke and wrote in Greek during the time of the early church.

HITTITES—These people lived to the north of Israel in the region of Syria.

MOABITES—Genesis 19 tells the story of Lot, Abraham's nephew, who had an incestuous relationship with his daughter. The resulting son, Moab, became the father of these people who lived east of the Jordan. A constant enemy of Israel, the Moabites joined forces with the Ammonites during the time of the judges (Judges 3). Later, the people of Moab fought a number of battles against the Northern and Southern Kingdoms (2 Kings 1, 3; 2 Chronicles 20).

MEDES AND PERSIANS—These people lived in the region known as modern day Iran. While originally two distinct people groups, the Medes dominated the Persians and together they defeated the Babylonians, Assyrians, and the Jewish people under the Mede leadership of King Darius (Daniel 5:31). Eventually, however, the Persians usurped the Medes and retained the throne. It was under the reign of the Persians that the Bible records events that occurred under King Cyrus (2 Chronicles 36; Ezra 1). Later, the Persian king Xerxes chose Esther to be his queen (Esther 1). The Persians were ultimately conquered by Alexander the Great of Greece.

ADDITIONAL INFORMATION:

Key Cities in Israel

Below is a list of key biblical cities and some of the events that occurred in those cities. Because the history of biblical Israel lasted over a thousand years, the atmosphere, culture, and personality (and sometimes even the exact location) of the cities changed significantly during that time.

BEERSHEBA—This city, along the southern end of Israel, was an important sanctuary for the people living near the Negev. Because this strategic city was in the southern region, it was often referred to as Israel's southern border. The Bible often refers to the land of Israel as stretching "from Dan to Beersheba" (2 Samuel 3:10). It was also the place where Abraham camped, dug a well, and banished Hagar and Ishmael (Genesis 21).

BETHEL—The first significant biblical event that occurred in Bethel was when God appeared to Jacob (Genesis 35). When Israel divided into two kingdoms, Bethel was toward the southern end of the Northern Kingdom. King Jeroboam used this strategic location to build one of two high places for worship—the other was built in Dan (1 Kings 12).

BETHANY—This city was important during Jesus' ministry. It was the home of Mary, Martha, and Lazarus— and the location Jesus raised Lazarus from the dead (John 11). It was the city where Jesus spent most of His final week as well as the location of His ascension into heaven (Luke 24).

BETHLEHEM—While known as the birthplace of Jesus (Luke 2), this was also the city where Ruth and Boaz met and were married (Ruth 2, 4). It also was the birthplace of King David (1 Samuel 16).

CANA—While the exact location of Cana is uncertain, the town was certainly located near Nazareth where Jesus and His mother lived. When they were invited to a wedding at Cana, Jesus and Mary attended the event where Jesus performed His first miracle (John 2).

CAPERNAUM—This city became one of the centers of Jesus' teaching ministry. A practical choice, it was the hometown of about half of Jesus' disciples and was located on some strategic trade routes—allowing a great number of people exposure to Jesus and His teaching.

DAN—This city was at the northernmost end of Israel and served as a convenient border and point of reference, just as Beersheba did in the south. When the Northern Kingdom became independent by rebelling against the line of David, King Jeroboam created a worship center in an effort to deter his citizens from journeying to Jerusalem to worship (1 Kings 12).

DOTHAN—When Jacob sent his son Joseph to check on his other brothers, Joseph went to Dothan where he was sold into slavery (Genesis 37). Centuries later, the army of Aram surrounded the city in a futile effort to capture Elisha (2 Kings 6).

EN GEDI—David hid from King Saul at En Gedi. Once while David was hiding in a cave, King Saul unknowingly entered the same cave to relieve himself. David cut off part of Saul's robe but left the king unharmed to prove that he had no intention of killing him though he had an easy opportunity (1 Samuel 24).

GILEAD—East of the Jordan River there is a twenty-mile strip of lush land well-suited for grazing animals. In addition to pasturelands, parts of the region are also heavily forested. This is a location where many people in the Bible found refuge, including Jacob and David. It was also in this forest that Absalom's hair became tangled in a tree before he was killed (2 Samuel 17–18).

HEBRON—Hebron became Abraham's home after he parted ways with his nephew, Lot, as recorded in Genesis 13. Also located here is the traditional site of Abraham's tomb (Genesis 23). It was here that King David established his first capital city before relocating it to Jerusalem (2 Samuel 2).

JERICHO—The city of Jericho is best known for the battle that occurred when the Israelites marched around the city for seven days before the walls crashed down (Joshua 6). Centuries later, the city was rebuilt and history tells us that the city became the winter home of King Herod. Other well-known Bible characters had a home here, including blind Bartimaeus and Zacchaeus (Mark 10; Luke 19).

JERUSALEM—The "city of David" had a long history and was occupied for at least two thousand years before David conquered it and made it his capital. Throughout the history of the Southern Kingdom, Jerusalem was the political and spiritual center of Israelite life and hosted the temple and the kings' palaces. The city has been destroyed and rebuilt many times over the years. At the time of Jesus, the city was home to a new temple built by Herod. Jerusalem was also the location of Jesus' crucifixion.

JOPPA—The prophet Jonah started his trip from Joppa when running from God's instruction (Jonah 1:3). This was also the city where Peter raised Tabitha from the dead and had a vision instructing him to eat non-kosher food (Acts 9–11).

NAZARETH—This small and insignificant community was the boyhood home of Jesus. Its obscurity helps explain Nathanael's bewilderment when he learned Jesus' hometown: "Can anything good come from there?" (John 1:46).

SAMARIA—In Jesus' day, the word Samaria referred to a region where many people of mixed ethnic descent lived. (Jesus used this fact to illustrate the kindness of the Good Samaritan in Luke 10.) Before Jesus' day, however, Samaria referred to a city that was forty miles north of Jerusalem. King Omri of the Northern Kingdom established the city and made it his capital (1 Kings 16).

SHECHEM—Shechem was the site of many important events in the history of the people of Israel. It was here that God appeared to Abraham and promised to give him the land of Canaan (Genesis 12:6–7). It was also the location where the people renewed their allegiance to God under Joshua (Joshua 24). Later, this city became a city of refuge and served as a capital city for the Northern Kingdom.

TYRE—Tyre was a city located fourteen miles north of the border of Israel, yet was an important city to King David and King Solomon. Without a strategic seaport within the borders of Israel, the kings of Israel fostered good relationships with the people of Tyre, which allowed them to move many goods through their seaport (1 Kings 5).

ADDITIONAL INFORMATION:

Water in Israel

Since the terrain of Israel can change from lush green to harsh wilderness within a few miles, it is understandable why water became such an important image to the biblical writers. Since much of the land of Israel is in a dry region, the work of digging wells and cisterns became incredibly important, and this work is often referred to in the Old Testament narratives. The areas of dry climate also yielded many powerful, poetic images such as Psalm 42:1: "As the deer pants for streams of water, so my soul pants for you, O God."

While a portion of Israel maintains a dry climate, there are also areas of the country that are quite wet and green. Below are some of the key bodies of water located within the boundaries of Israel.

THE SEA OF GALILEE is fourteen miles long, yet only three to four miles wide. Located in the northern portion of the land, this lake had many towns surrounding it. This freshwater lake provided necessary water for the region as well as fish for food. Many of Jesus' disciples were fishermen and would have carried out their trade on this lake. In the Old Testament, this body of water was called the Sea of Kinnereth (Numbers 34:10; Joshua 13:27). Today, it is referred to as Lake Tiberias or Lake Kinneret.

THE JORDAN RIVER is a 156-mile river that runs from the northern region near the Sea of Galilee and empties into the salty Dead Sea. This river runs in a generally southern direction and provides much of the land with fresh water. The Jordan River was the location of many miracles in the Bible, including miraculous crossings by Joshua, Elijah, and Elisha (Joshua 3; 2 Kings 2). It was also the location where Naaman bathed and was cleansed of leprosy (2 Kings 5), and where Jesus was baptized by John the Baptist (Matthew 3). Today the Jordan River helps form borders between Israel and her neighbors. Its depth has been reduced because of irrigation projects completed by the countries of Israel and Jordan.

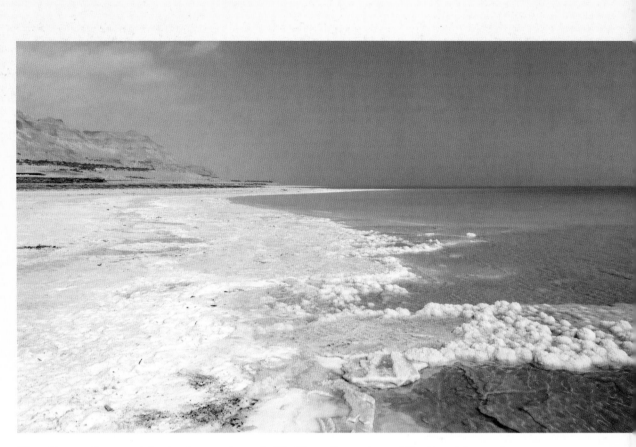

THE DEAD SEA is a lake in the southern half of Israel's territory. The Dead Sea is forty-two miles long and at its greatest breadth eleven miles wide. This salt lake is nearly nine times saltier than the ocean. The only tributary into the Dead Sea is the Jordan River, and there are no streams or water outlets that lead out of the Dead Sea. In addition, the region itself only receives two to four inches of rain per year. While the Dead Sea served as a useful border between the lands of Israel, Moab, and Edom, it is said that Solomon, Aristotle, Herod, and the Queen of Sheba all enjoyed using the mineral-rich waters from the Dead Sea for medicinal purposes. The picture on this page is from the shores of this salt sea.

THE MEDITERRANEAN SEA (also called "The Great Sea" or "The Sea") borders Israel, much of southern Europe, and northern Africa. This body of water helped connect Israel to the rest of the known world. Solomon used it to float timbers of cedar from Lebanon for his building projects near Jerusalem as well as to expand Israel's economy (1 Kings 5). Paul traveled it extensively, bringing the message of Christianity to many of the cities that bordered the Sea.

ADDITIONAL INFORMATION:

Jewish Calendar

The traditional Hebrew calendar mentioned in the Bible uses different months than we are used to in our Western culture, which follows the Gregorian calendar system. In most of the Bible, the months are referred to by their number (for example, "in the fourth month"). When the Jewish people returned from exile, however, they began to call months by specific Babylonian names. And while the first month of the Jewish year is Nisan, the Jewish New Year is actually celebrated in the seventh month. That may seem unusual to our modern system—but we have our own similar anomalies (such as starting a new school year in September). Below is a list of Jewish months with their Gregorian equivalents.

MONTH	HEBREW MONTH	WHEN IT OCCURS IN THE GREGORIAN CALENDAR
1st month	Nisan	March–April
2nd month	Iyar	April–May
3rd month	Sivan	May–June
4th month	Tammuz	June–July
5th month	Ab	July–August
6th month	Elul	August–September
7th month	Tishri	September–October
8th month	Heshvan	October–November
9th month	Chislev	November–December
10th month	Tebeth	December–January
11th month	Shebat	January–February
12th month	Adar	February–March

Table of Weights and Measures

BIBLE	AMERICAN/ BRITISH	METRIC
MEASURES OF LENGTH		
cubit	1.5 feet	0.46 meter
span	9 inches	22.9 centimeters
handbreadth	3 inches	7.6 centimeters
reed (or measuring rod or fathom)	9 feet	2.7 meters
a sabbath's day journey	0.5 mile	0.8 kilometer
a day's journey	24 miles	38.6 kilometers
MEASURES OF WEIGHT (CURRENCY)		
talent	75 pounds	34 kilograms
mina	1.2 pounds	0.5 kilogram
shekel	0.4 ounce	10.2 grams
drachma	0.3 ounce	7.7 grams
bekah	0.2 ounce	5.2 grams
gerah	0.02 ounce	0.6 gram
MEASURES OF DRY GOODS		
cor (or homer)	6.2 bushels	220 liters
ephah	0.5 bushels	18.2 liters
seah	6.4 quarts	6.1 liters
omer	1.9 quarts	1.8 liters
MEASURES OF LIQUID GOODS		
bath	5.8 gallons	21.9 liters
hin	1 gallon	3.8 liters
log	0.3 quart	0.3 liter

To find the value of money in terms of today's currency, multiply the money's weight against the current values of gold and silver. For example, to find the value of a silver shekel, multiply 0.4 ounces against the today's trading rate of silver.

While this table provides good estimates, biblical scholars often differ on the exact figures of each measurement.

THE HOLY LAND
TODAY

0   5   10   20   30 Miles
0 5 10   20   30   40 Km

LEBANON

GOLAN
HEIGHTS
*(occupied
by Israel)*

SYRIA

*Sea of
Galilee*

Mediterranean Sea

Jordan River

WEST
BANK

GAZA
STRIP

Dead Sea

ISRAEL

JORDAN

EGYPT

SAUDI
ARABIA

N

Copyright © 2007 by Barbour Publishing, Inc.

Satellite photo of the Holy Land today.

ABOUT THE CONTRIBUTORS

DAVID BARRETT is a freelance Bible reference editor and cartographer. His love for the Bible and his training in editing, ancient languages, and computer programming have cultivated a lasting fascination with Bible geography and the illumination it brings to scripture. Along with professional Bible maps and resources, David has developed Bible Mapper software (www.biblemapper.com), a tool that enables users to create very accurate, customized maps of Bible lands or research a particular aspect of Bible history and geography. David lives in Chambersburg, Pennsylvania, with his wife, Anisea, and their three children.

TODD BOLEN is Associate Professor of Biblical Studies at the Israel Bible Extension campus of The Master's College. Since 1996, he has lived in Israel and taught college and seminary students about biblical sites and history. His passion for teaching and photography led him to develop the Pictorial Library of Bible Lands, a collection of six thousand high-resolution images on a series of ten CDs. Todd's photographs have been published in hundreds of books and magazines and featured on CNN and NationalGeographic.com. When not teaching in the classroom or trekking about the Middle East, Todd loves spending time with his wife and four children. More information about his photographic collections and the latest news about biblical lands is available at http://www.BiblePlaces.com.

CHRISTOPHER D. HUDSON has contributed to over fifty Bible projects, sixty study guides, and a hundred books. Best-sellers include the *Inspirational Bible* (more than a million sold), *The Extreme Teen Bible* (more than a million sold), and the *Revolution Bible*. Chris consulted or contributed to projects for every major Bible translation launch within the last thirteen years: The New Living Translation, God's Word, The English Standard Version, The Holman Christian Standard Bible, and the Today's New International Version. He lives in Northern Illinois with his wife and three children.